SHOWERS

BY
BEVERLY CLARK

THE COMPLETE GUIDE TO HOSTING A PERFECT BRIDAL OR BABY SHOWER

WILSHIRE PUBLICATIONS

Cover design: Burke Design
China: Richard Ginori

Illustrations by Karen Bell
Editor: Celine Burk

Published by Wilshire Publications,
Beverly Clark Collection
Carpinteria, CA

Distributed by:
        Book Trade — Publishers Group West, Emeryville, CA
        Gift Trade —   Cogan Books, Fullerton, CA
                    Beverly Clark Collection
                    6385 B. Rose Lane
                    Carpinteria, CA 93013
                    (800) 888-6866

ISBN 0-934081-03-4

Library of Congress Cataloging - in Publication Data
1. Clark, Beverly   II. Showers

To my husband, for his encouragement, support, and understanding.

Acknowledgments

I would like to thank my staff Mary Jo Keller, Jon Swift, Premilla Ram for their dedicated work which allowed me the time to write this book, and to Jolaine Overos for sharing her recipes and ideas.

With special thanks to my editor Celine Burk for her expertise and tireless efforts to help make this book a pleasure to read.

Contents

Introduction

When hosting a shower for a close friend or relative, whether it be your first time or your fiftieth, you will want it to be as special as the person you're giving it for.

With a little additional thought and attention to detail, you can turn what might otherwise be just another ordinary shower into a smashing success. Surprise your guests with imaginative decorations, challenging games, and delightful party favors.

There is more to creating a memorable event than tasty food and fabulous decorations. A successful party also depends on your ability to make your guests feel completely at ease. This is accomplished by a hostess who is prepared and organized. Use the tips, checklists and worksheets provided to help you prevent oversights and frantic last minute rushing.

Choose from a number of shower themes, or combine portions of a few and design a shower that is uniquely yours. This book is intended to give you creative ideas that will spark your own imagination so you can assemble an affair that will reflect your taste and that of the bride or mother-to-be.

HOSTING
A SHOWER

Chapter 1

HOSTING A SHOWER

The History of a Cherished Tradition

*T*he first bridal shower was said to have taken place in Holland when a young girl fell in love with a poor but generous miller. Over the years the miller had given away all his possessions to those needier than himself so that when the time came to wed he had nothing left to offer his prospective bride.

Furious with his daughter's choice of suitors, her father forbade the marriage and refused the young pair the customary dowry, which was necessary to establish a household. Without it the pair had little hope of being able to begin a life together. It was then that the community came to the couple's rescue. Out of appreciation for the miller's benevolence, his friends banded together and literally "showered" the young girl with all the items necessary to set up a house. It was the beginning of a long marriage and a beautiful tradition.

Who Hosts a Shower

A vestige of the old-fashioned dowry each bride received from her family, the bridal shower has remained a special gift given the bride by her "family of friends." The party is customarily hosted by the Maid of Honor or the Bridesmaids. It may also be held by a relative, close friend, or even co-worker, of either the bride-to-be or her mother. Formerly, strict rules of etiquette precluded the mother or sister of the bride from serving as hostess since presents are expected. More recently, however, this rule has been relaxed and there are areas of the country where it is not only acceptable but quite customary for the immediate family to hold the shower. As in most matters concerning etiquette, it is best to know what is accepted in your own community and then decide how closely you wish to follow local custom. Even if immediate family members do not host the event itself, they may wish to be included by either helping to defray some of the costs involved or by offering their home as a location for the party. If the ladies in the bridal party are jointly hosting the shower, the responsibilities should be evenly divided. One individual, usually the Maid of Honor or the one whose home is used, acts as the shower coordinator.

It is not necessary to be invited to the wedding in order to host a shower. This is particularly true if you are a co-worker or business associate who wants to celebrate this special event but are not close enough friends with the bride to be invited to her wedding.

Hosting a Shower for the Second-time Bride

Since the original purpose of a wedding shower was to help the bride set up her first household, showers generally were not held for the bride who was remarrying. Today the original intent of the event has generally been disregarded, with showers for the second-time bride being held in the spirit of a prenuptial party for the pair. Although formality and style may vary, these showers are usually simpler. In keeping with the tone of a second marriage ceremony, the shower is smaller with less elaborate decorations. In addition, gifts tend to be of a more personal nature rather than items for the household.

Who's Invited

Since bridal showers tend to be more intimate occasions than weddings, usually only the closest of friends and relatives are invited. The exception is the party given by an office staff, sorority, or club. Formerly, bridal showers were women-only, afternoon gatherings which tended to adhere to the same format. Now, changing times have given this affair an updated look with the only limit being your imagination. As the average age of bridal couples has increased, so has the participation of men in all aspects of the wedding and its accompanying festivities. No longer strictly for women, bridal showers now place a new emphasis on couples. Co-ed showers, which honor both the bride and groom are increasingly in demand with both evening parties and barbecues lending themselves nicely to this now popular option.

If there will be two or more showers held, make sure that the guest list is not redundant. With the exception of the immediate family, the same guest should be invited to only one or two parties at the most. To avoid straining the pocketbooks of those attending two showers, you may want to emphasize to these prospective guests that their presence at the second shower is enough of a gift. For those who might still feel uncomfortable coming "empty-handed," a few fresh flowers from the garden would be a welcomed addition to the festive table. If you know the other people who are also planning to host a shower, you may want to get in touch with them about the possibility of combining parties and co-hosting one large party in place of several smaller ones. It's a great way to ease some of the burden placed on the hostess and avoid duplication of guest lists.

Keeping in mind both your budget and the number of guests your prospective location will comfortably accommodate, tentatively establish the number you wish to invite. Then consult with the bride regarding the guest list. Most showers have between 10 and 30 guests with co-ed parties having as many as 40 celebrants. If you are hosting a surprise shower, contact the bride's mother and/or her fiancé to get the wedding guest list. Also ask for the names and addresses of special friends and relatives who should be included.

Usually those invited to the shower will also be attending the wedding. There are exceptions, however, such as in the case of the office or club-sponsored shower. Also small "family-only" or out-of-town ceremonies will naturally limit the number of shower guests who will also be present at the nuptials.

The Invitation

Unless the invitations are to be extended informally by telephone, the hostess should mail them out no later than three to four weeks before the shower. Handwritten invitations are generally preferred except in the case of a small shower with only very close friends or an informal, last minute get together.

The wide variety of preprinted invitations currently available, as well as the freedom to use your own creative ideas, can insure that your invitation reflects and reinforces the style or theme of your special event. In most cases, the pertinent information is handwritten. Try a touch of calligraphy to add creative flair. For a large, elegant shower, such as a co-ed cocktail party or formal dinner, you may prefer to have the entire invitation custom printed.

What to Include

Whether you use a preprinted invitation or one of your own design, be sure to include the following:

- Name of the host or hostess. When the entire bridal party is hosting the shower, you may either list the individual names or simply state "given by the bridal party."

- Name of the person the shower is honoring.

- The date and time of day.

- The address.

- Travel directions. A must for those not familiar with the location, you should be sure to include a separate piece of paper with a small map or clear directions. Don't forget to include the telephone number of the house or facility where the party will take place, just in case someone gets lost on the way.

- RSVP with a telephone number. To ensure more responses, you may opt to include a deadline for replies.

Additional Information

You may want to include any or all of the following somewhere on your invitation:

- The shower theme (kitchen, lingerie, etc.)

- Special requirements of your particular shower. In the case of an Around-the-clock shower, for example, you need to designate the specific time of day each guest has been assigned and what this means (SEE SHOWER THEMES.) If you are having a recipe shower, don't forget to include a recipe card with instructions on how you want it to be filled out. In the case of a surprise shower, be sure to emphasize it on the invitation.

- Practical information to help your guests in selecting a gift. Guests should know exactly which colors and accessories the bride has selected for her decor, as well as where she is registered. In the case of a lingerie shower, don't forget to include her size! Searching for the perfect present can quickly become a burden to those with busy schedules. Do your guests a favor by encouraging the bride to register at a local store which carries items appropriate for your shower. It reduces the guesswork by clearly stating the bride's taste and preferences and also helps avoid the embarrassment of two guests showing up with the same gift

Wording and Style Depend on You — Some Examples:

Formal printed invitation:

Karen and Andrew Smith

invite you to attend a bridal shower

in honor of

Carolyn Evans and John Spencer

Saturday, June tenth at five o'clock

720 Maple Avenue

RSVP   *Kitchen Shower*
361-5992

Less formal bridal shower invitation:

You're invited to a bridal shower!

For: Rhonda Crowell

Date: Saturday, June 10th Time: 12:00 noon

Place: 720 El Medio Road

Pacific Palisades

Given by: Donna Cowen and Debbie Jones

RSVP: (213) 494-7737 by May 27th

It's a kitchen shower!

The Creative Invitation

First impressions are important so choose your invitation carefully. It will set the mood for the theme and style of shower you have chosen. A unique and creative invitation is not only more fun to make but also more fun to receive. It's great to capture the interest of your guests from the moment they read it!

Here are just a few ideas to spark your imagination:

Rain or Shine — You will need to purchase either large fabric umbrellas or small paper ones (one for each guest invited) and a supply of fabric paints in complimentary colors. Working with the umbrellas open, write the party details across a section of the material. When the paint is thoroughly dry, fold the umbrellas and slip into cardboard tubes for mailing.

The Sweetheart Box — Each invitation will require a heart-shaped helium balloon (available at specialty and party stores), one yard of curling ribbon, and a white gift box slightly larger than the inflated balloon. Using colorful magic markers, write out the invitation on the balloon and tie a ribbon to it tightly. Tape the other end of the ribbon securely to the inside of the container. After your balloon "invitation" is nestled in the box, tape the lid down. These unique pop-up surprises should be hand-delivered to the doorstep of each guest.

Around-the-clock Fun — In keeping with the theme of an Around-the-clock shower (SEE THEMES), cut individual alarm clocks out of colored construction paper. You can use either a single sheet or a folded piece of paper, if you want the alarm clock to open. Write the shower details either on the back of each clock or inside, if you have chosen the folded style. Now you are ready to personalize the invitations. On each alarm clock, draw a face depicting a different time of day according to the time you've assigned each guest. These alarm clocks set the mood for the shower where each person brings a gift appropriate for the individually designated time of day.

Kitchen Keepsake — For the kitchen shower, buy or make individual potholders or kitchen towels. Print out the shower information with fabric paint and you've just created a memorable addition to your friends' kitchens!

An Elegant Note — Select fine notecards and write out your invitation. If you or a friend knows calligraphy, it can add to the overall elegance of your cards. Glue small satin bows in the top corners of the cards or punch two holes on the left hand side, thread a length of satin ribbon through each and tie in a festive bow. Glitter or confetti scattered in the envelope will lend a festive air to your creation.

It's a Puzzle — Enlarge a picture of the happy couple to 5 x 7" and order enough copies to send one to each guest. Glue each

8

picture onto a piece of thin white cardboard. When dry, write out the invitation on the back of each picture, then cut into irregular "puzzle" pieces. Each puzzle can be mailed in its own regular size envelope.

Baker's Special — Bake oversized decorator cookies (SEE PERSONALIZED INITIAL COOKIES) and write party details in frosting. This is a fun preview of a tea or dessert shower.

Sweet Temptation — As a prelude to a very formal dessert party, buy quality chocolates specially packaged in tiny gold boxes. Make or order your invitations in black or white and gold to coordinate with the foil containers. Place each invitation on top of its own box and secure with a lacy gold ribbon.

The Delicate Touch — Buy individual fans to use as "cards" on which to write your summons to a Victorian tea.

Bon Voyage — A honeymoon shower needs a special invitation. Use construction paper to fashion a travel ticket or select picture postcards to set the stage for your shower "adventure."

Linen Closet Cabaret — Use a linen or plain cloth napkin as a stunning background on which to paint the particulars of your linen or kitchen shower.

Creative Cut-Outs — Use brightly-colored construction paper, wallpaper samples, or scraps of fabric to cut into shapes to suit your fancy. Hearts, bells, and doves are just a few of the designs you can use to create a truly unique invitation to go along with your decorations.

SHOWER GUEST LIST

Name	Street, City, State, Zip	Phone	Reply

10

SHOWER GUEST LIST

Name	Street, City, State, Zip	Phone	Reply

SHOWER GUEST LIST

Name	Street, City, State, Zip	Phone	Reply

PLANNING
A
BRIDAL
SHOWER

Chapter 2

PLANNING A BRIDAL SHOWER

*A*ll good parties involve work and the bridal shower is no exception! Planning a memorable party and having fun doing so, should be your goal. Since a bridal shower takes the coordination of what may seem to be an endless number of small details, you need to start with a realistic assessment of your resources. Doing this before you begin makes the entire process easier and avoids unnecessary complications later on. First you need to decide what you can afford in terms of time and money. Then consider what other resources are available to you, including invaluables such as space, equipment, and talented or energetic friends! Knowing what you have to work with can help you begin to find the sort of celebration that is the perfect reflection of the guest of honor and your own personal style.

Setting the Date

Unless a surprise party is on the agenda, the hostess usually consults with the bride and perhaps the groom before finalizing the date. It's always preferable to have your guest of honor at the celebration! So, be sure to check before going ahead with a definite date.

Somewhere between four to six weeks prior to the wedding itself is a good time to hold a shower. This may vary according to individual schedules and the number of showers being held. In the case of several celebrations, be sure to double-check with the other hostesses or the bride herself to avoid planning your event for the same weekend as another party. Also, make sure that the time schedule you have set is realistic. Do you have enough time to prepare everything? Is there plenty of time to mail out the invitations with enough leeway for replies? Depending on the type of shower, you may need more time than you had originally planned on. Look at all the aspects, take possible scheduling conflicts into consideration, and then set a date that you can comfortably meet.

Don't forget to think about the guests you will be inviting. If most of them work, a weekend luncheon might be easier to schedule than a party during the week. If most of the guests coming to an all-women shower are married, you might have a better turn-out by selecting a weekday evening as opposed to a weekend evening when many couples have social obligations. That same weekend evening, however, is a great choice for a co-ed shower. It's a matter of knowing what type of shower you want and who you're inviting.

Choosing the Type of Shower and the Time of Day

Once you have set the date, you need to select an appropriate time of day. This is largely determined by the type of shower you will be giving, the guest list, and your budget.

First Things First:

- What's your estimated budget?
- How large do you want the party to be?
- Are you going to make it co-ed?
- Look outside! How is the weather, warm or cold?
- Is it a surprise?

Working through the above should get you ready to sift through the various types of parties to find the one that best suits your style and circumstances.

Keep in mind both your expertise and your limitations. Plan a party that you can comfortably handle and will enjoy giving. If cooking is not your forte, it is wise not to commit yourself to a sit-down dinner for 40 unless you can afford to have it catered (you still get all the credit!) Once you've been realistic and carefully considered and established your limits, then you can get ready for the fun by letting your imagination and creativity safely run wild!

Types of Affairs and Their Appropriate Hours

A Brunch

Generally held on a weekend morning, a brunch is usually called for 10:00 or 11:00 AM and can be expected to last into the early afternoon. A good choice for either all-female or co-ed showers, a brunch can be either sit-down or buffet style. Often chosen because of its flexibility, this type of meal may take place indoors or out, being as formal or informal as you wish. Its versatility will accommodate even the most modest of budgets.

A Luncheon

The luncheon has an air of a ladies-only outing. Either a home or a restaurant is the appropriate setting for this type of event, which is usually slated to begin between noon and 1:00 PM. Whether offering table service or a buffet, which can be slightly cheaper, the cost is moderate to expensive.

An Afternoon Tea

Usually set for between 2:00 and 5:00 PM, but commencing no later than 3:30 PM, this affair is best reserved for ladies only. A tea can not only be a delightful change of pace but can also be relatively inexpensive, as well.

A Cocktail Party

With its air of sophistication, the cocktail party is perfect for the co-ed celebration. It also provides the ideal solution to space and budgetary limitations. You can do a lot with a little for this one! Cocktails are served between 4:00 and 7:00 PM.

A Dinner Party

A dinner party can be quite versatile, everything from an all-ladies potluck buffet to an elegant sit-down dinner for couples. You can opt for either a weekday or weekend evening with a starting time anywhere from 5:00 to 7:00 PM. The cost will range from moderate to expensive.

A Dessert Party

Everyone loves sweets and there's no better place to indulge than at this tempting affair. A dessert party can be a mid-afternoon ladies gathering or a co-ed event starting after dinner, at 7:30 or 8:00 PM. It's fun, relatively inexpensive and a sweet gesture for the couple-to-be!

Selecting a Location

In order to select a location that will enhance that special day, keep in mind the number of guests you want to invite, the type of party you want, the working budget, and the time of year. Also take into consideration any special locations you might have access to — country clubs, church halls, and club meeting rooms can all be kind to the limited budget.

Although most showers are given in the hostess's home, they may also be held in the home of the bride's mother or a relative, a restaurant or outdoor recreation area. Although a home tends to provide the coziest and most relaxed environment, a banquet room at a local hotel or club may be preferable for the larger shower. It's important to look at the space you have objectively in order to accurately estimate how many people you can comfortably entertain. If your guests will primarily be standing, as in the case of a cocktail party, the average room can generally accommodate 20 guests. A three room area consisting of living, dining and family rooms can hold about 40. Plan on rearranging furniture and removing bulky items temporarily to allow for a smooth flow of guests from one room to the next. This assures that the guests can mingle freely without traffic jams and tight corners. If you're planning on a buffet brunch, don't forget to consider available seating.

Be creative and flexible when it comes to looking at your options. Try to find a location that enhances the theme of your shower, rather than remaining a neutral backdrop. On the other hand, be willing to adjust your theme to fit a great location. If you're holding a summer shower and your choice of locations has been narrowed down to the beach or local park, why not enhance the setting by opting for a Hawaiian luau or Western barbecue? Try to utilize the community you live in by checking with your local Parks and Recreation Authority for available sites. Before settling on one, however, make sure that you are up-to-date on whether a permit is required, if fires and alcoholic beverages are allowed, and how parking and traffic are managed. Another great resource is your local historical society. Just imagine staging a Victorian Tea in the quaint garden of a Victorian mansion! The possibilities are endless, it just takes a little legwork to find out what your options are.

In making a final decision on location, keep the overall budget in mind. A home shower, whether indoors or out in the garden, will be less costly than one held at a club or restaurant.

Determining Your Budget

A good place to start, if you're hosting a shower by yourself, is by taking a careful look at your own finances. What can you comfortably afford to spend? With the knowledge of your location and the length of your guest list, begin by writing down everything you think you will need to carry off the event you're planning. Use the checklist provided to make sure you haven't overlooked a small but costly detail. If you see that you are beginning to leave your original budget far behind, stop and regroup! Budgets can be saved! You can cut down the number of guests or modify the style of the shower. For example, if you had planned on hosting a sit-down luncheon calling for the rental of tables, linens, and chairs, consider changing to an afternoon tea serving dainty finger sandwiches and desserts, where only napkins or small paper plates are necessary.

The best way to work on a limited budget is to have a co-hostess (even better, if it is the entire bridal party!) Have a general meeting to determine the budget and divide the responsibilities. The money can be pooled with one or two people acting as the shoppers for items the group has already agreed upon, or each person can be assigned things to purchase. Either way, be sure to write down who's responsible for what to avoid confusion as you get closer to the date.

Try to keep costs to a minimum by borrowing things you don't have from a friend. Rather than renting china, feel free to use the beautiful paper or plastic plates available.

Budget Tips

- Hold the party at your home or in a friend's backyard.
- Decide on a brunch, afternoon tea, or dessert party.
- Buy food and/or liquor from a wholesale outlet.
- Eliminate alcohol in favor of exotic fruit punch.
- Hire students to help set up, serve, and tend bar.
- When going formal, check with your local hotel and restaurant management school for competent but less expensive waiters, bartenders, and catering help.
- Create your own floral arrangement or centerpieces, concentrating on the flowers currently in season. In winter, choose dried flowers for centerpieces.
- Balloons can be the budget decorator's best friend—colorful and versatile, they won't deplete your finances!

SECRETS FOR A SUCCESSFUL SHOWER

Chapter 3

SECRETS FOR A
SUCCESSFUL SHOWER

*T*he secret to a successful party is all in the organization. Let a few tips be your guide to making your shower the best and most enjoyable it can possibly be! And remember, by doing things in time, you will be the best kind of hostess there is — a relaxed one.

Shower Tips

General Tips to Get You Going

- Go with the kind of party you do best. As simple as this seems, many hostesses get carried away and end up over their heads with a party that just isn't feasible. Accept your limitations and respect your budget, the capacity of your home, and the availability of equipment and help.

- Don't just admire the checklist and work sheets provided, use them! Rely on your pencil and not on your memory — write it down!!

- Follow the checklist furnished as your master plan to avoid leaving things to the very last minute.

- Check silver, linens, and any necessary supplies well ahead of time.

- Go over the seating possibilities and make sure that you have enough chairs and space for the number of guests.

- Consider choosing a party theme. Theme celebrations are usually fun and definitely more memorable (SEE CHAPTER ON THEMES.)

Now-that-you're-on-your-way Tips

- If you have chosen to have a theme, coordinate the invitations, food, decorations, and party favors. You want your theme to be a focal point and not merely an afterthought.

- Try to invite guests who know each other or at least one other person. Otherwise there will be too much pressure on you (and the guest of honor) during the party.

- Plan games and activities that will appeal to your guests. Games can turn an ordinary party into a special event.

- Select party favors that are different. Unique items are more fun for your guests.

- If you think you will need help to carry off the party with style, by all means, get it! Ask a friend or turn to one of the many professional agencies for special help. Students can also be your saving grace when it comes to food preparation, serving, and clean-up.

- Plan on keeping the menu manageable so that you will be free to enjoy yourself along with your guests! Stay away from time-consuming dishes and remember, this is NOT the time to experiment, no matter what your Aunt Martha says!

- In calculating the amount of food you will need, overestimate cheerfully. It's always better to have leftovers than to run short. To prevent food from getting cold, plan on borrowing or renting chafing dishes and hot plates.

Basics Not To Forget

- Buy film for your camera ahead of time.

- Assign the role of photographer to someone who knows which end of the camera should be facing forward. Chances are you yourself will get sidetracked. Terrific shots can later be made into a special momento for the bride.

- Have your guest bathroom well-stocked with the niceties party-goers appreciate — guest soaps, hand towels, lotion, and an extra roll of toilet tissue.

- Make your powder room special by adding fresh flowers, scented potpourri, and, for evening, a lit candle, to make your guests feel pampered.

- Get all of the cleaning and most of the cooking out of the way ahead of time, and try not to leave anything until the last minute.

More Basics Closer to the Date

- Decide now if you want to give the bride a corsage since it must be ordered in advance.

- Select a "gift corner" where the bride will be able to sit in full view of all her friends as she opens her gifts.

- Plan seating so that it will help, not hinder, conversation.

- If you are serving buffet-style, be sure to scatter tray tables around the room or give each guest a lap tray for her food.

- Inexpensive but charming wicker lap trays can be purchased for each guest and then given as a favor to take home.

- Be a little daring in your seating arrangement for a sit-down dinner. Separate spouses, placing each one next to someone new.

- Choose creative ways to serve your food to add a festive note to your table (SEE TABLE SETTINGS.)

- Create the atmosphere you're after through the skillful use of lighting, music, and decorations. Whether lively, elegant, or cozy, there's a mood to fit your party — experiment with the options in advance until you hit on the right combination.

- Smoothly-run parties have definite stages that can be planned in advance. Be aware of the time and how your guests are feeling as indications that they may be ready for the next stage.

- The beginning of a party can be awkward. Ask a few close friends to arrive early so that the first guest steps into a lively atmosphere.

- Above all, be ready on time!

SHOWER CHECKLIST

Six to Eight Weeks Before

- ☐ Discuss your plans for hosting a shower with the bride. Go over the guest list, date and theme.

- ☐ If it's a surprise shower, contact the bride's mother and fiancé to let them know your plans and to obtain the wedding guest list.

- ☐ Once the date is set, be sure that the bride's mother, the groom, and anyone else involved in planning the shower knows the chosen date and time.

- ☐ If there is more than one hostess, hold a meeting to discuss theme, location, and budget, and to divide the duties.

- ☐ Draw up the guest list.

- ☐ If it is not an at-home affair, look for a banquet room at a hotel, restaurant, or club and reserve it immediately (this may require a deposit.)

- ☐ Set a preliminary budget so that you have something to work with.

- ☐ Decide on a theme and the type and style of the shower you want to host.

- ☐ Make or buy appropriate invitations.

- ☐ Fill out the invitations and address the envelopes. Include an RSVP date, which should be one to two weeks prior to the event. Be sure you have given a telephone number.

- ☐ Think about decorating ideas and start browsing to see what's available. Good party supply and art stores are filled with great party items. Check rental companies, the yellow pages, and use your imagination for further ideas.

- ☐ If this is a joint shower, divide the decorating tasks and expenses. Deciding who will be responsible for doing what is almost as crucial as actually doing it!

- ☐ If you're using party help, reserve early — caterers, servers, and clean-up help can get booked up far in advance, especially during holiday seasons.

- ☐ Think about having entertainment. If you want to hire musicians, palm readers, magicians, or other entertainers, it is wise to find and book them immediately.

- ☐ If games are on the agenda, decide on which ones and start collecting everything you need.

Four to Six Weeks Before

☐ Determine the number and type of game prizes needed and start shopping for them.

☐ Purchase or make your party favors.

☐ Set your menu and gather the recipes needed.

☐ Begin your checklist of necessary equipment, food, and liquor.

☐ Reserve rental items.

☐ Purchase or make place cards. As soon as guests begin to confirm, fill in their names on the cards.

☐ Mail out the invitations (four weeks before.)

Three Weeks Before

☐ If there are other hostesses involved, call another meeting to check on everyone's progress and to assign food and beverage preparation chores.

☐ Make a detailed marketing list for food.

☐ Finish shopping for game equipment and prizes.

☐ Put the finishing touches on party favors, if necessary.

Two Weeks Before

☐ Assign a shower secretary to be in charge of recording who brought which gift. The same person can also make a ribbon "bridal bouquet" for the bride.

☐ Do all major cleaning, such as emptying coat closets.

☐ If the event is being held in a hotel or club, confirm your reservation. Also, finalize the menu with the staff coordinator.

☐ Order floral centerpieces.

☐ Touch base with the entertainers and caterers (or friends who have promised to bring food.)

☐ Wrap game prizes.

One Week Before

☐ Tally up the number of guests and call those who have not yet responded to see if they are planning to attend. This is especially critical for a sit-down meal.

☐ Prepare food that can be frozen ahead.

☐ Start decorating.

- ☐ Decide what you will wear and make sure that it is cleaned and pressed.
- ☐ Clean and polish the silver.
- ☐ Arrange for space in a neighbor's refrigerator, if needed.
- ☐ Clean the house.

Two Days Before

- ☐ Review the checklist to make sure that nothing has been overlooked.
- ☐ Check with the other hostesses to make sure that things have gone smoothly for them.
- ☐ Confirm delivery or pick-up time with your florist. Delivery should be set for early in the morning of your event.
- ☐ Collect everything you need to borrow — chairs, tables, and serving pieces.
- ☐ Make sure that all linens are ironed.
- ☐ Wash china and crystal.

The Day Before

- ☐ Make any food that can be safely stored overnight. Some foods, such as pasta salads, are actually better when made the day before.
- ☐ Clean the fruit and vegetables and get them ready for slicing.
- ☐ Recheck the delivery time of rental items.
- ☐ Set up chairs, tables with linens, and get out serving utensils and napkins.
- ☐ Finish last minute decorating and straightening up around the house.
- ☐ Make sure you have enough ice.
- ☐ Pick up flowers late in the day unless they are scheduled to be delivered the next morning.
- ☐ Set up an area to display the shower gifts.
- ☐ Last but not least — take a hot bath, relax, and get a good night's sleep!

The Day of the Shower

- ☐ Have another hostess or friend come early to help with last minute details.
- ☐ Finish preparing the food.
- ☐ Make punches, juices, etc.
- ☐ Place food on serving dishes and garnish.
- ☐ Get dressed.
- ☐ If serving snack or finger foods like nuts, chips and dip, or cheese and crackers, set them out just before your guests are scheduled to arrive.

The Party Itself

- ☐ Greet your guests with a smile, an offer of a drink, and introduce them to at least one other person.
- ☐ If this is a surprise shower, have the bride arrive a half hour after all the other guests. Appoint someone as look-out and get ready to shout "surprise!"
- ☐ When the bride makes her entrance, greet her with a corsage, lei, or other special favor you have planned for her.
- ☐ Proceed according to the timetable you have already planned.
- ☐ Remember to be aware of the time and the mood of the guests in deciding when to move onto the next activity. Do not rush your guests but don't leave them waiting and wondering what's next, either.
- ☐ Help the bride put her presents in her car.
- ☐ When the shower is being held at a restaurant, hotel, or club, plan on arriving in plenty of time to make any final arrangements. Count on doing last minute decorating, setting out place cards, arranging party favors, and being finished in enough time to greet the first guest with a smile!

SHOWER TIMETABLE

It is important to keep your party flowing so that it doesn't begin to drag. A slow pace can become boring, making the guests begin to get restless. Think of your party in three stages, allowing approximately 30 minutes to one hour for each. The exact length will depend on your guests.

First Stage

As guests arrive, introduce them to one another and serve drinks. You may want to have a few hors d'oeuvres, nuts or candies, but keep the snacks light so as not to spoil the meal! Although this is the time to socialize while waiting for everyone to arrive, you may want to start a quick game. Some games will be better suited than others but all will help break the ice and get people interacting.

Second Stage

This is when the food is served. If it is a complete meal, it is up to you whether you want to serve dessert immediately following or wait until after the gifts have been opened.

Third Stage

Now is the time for any games you might have planned. Activities can be a lot of fun and can make a good party great! In case there are too many guests and you feel that opening the presents will take a long time, you may want to skip having games or select ones to be played only in the first stage of the party. If you have not yet served coffee and cake, either have guests enjoy it while the presents are being opened or wait until the guest of honor has opened all her gifts.

Party favors that are not part of the place setting are given to the guests as they are preparing to leave. You can have them ready on a small table in the entrance hall.

DECORATIONS AND TABLE SETTINGS

Chapter 4

DECORATIONS AND TABLE SETTINGS

Decorations and table settings are vital to the mood and character of any festivity, so both should be carefully planned to complement the theme and style of your party. Decorations can run the gamut from very simple to extremely elaborate. What is important is the continuity of style.

Parties are really theatrical productions and you are the director. Decide how you want the stage to look and choose an appropriate setting, a delicious menu, interesting accessories and entertainment, add the spice of fun-loving guests, and you are guaranteed to have a smash success on your hands!

Decorating with Imagination

Indulge your imagination to create just the right atmosphere. If you prefer a formal, elegant style of shower without a particular theme, then beautiful flowers, candles, linens, and food arrangements can tastefully convey an atmosphere of sophisticated refinement. If, on the other hand, you're in search of an intimate, cozy setting for a "Pasta Party" you may want to recreate a little Italian bistro. Use red and white checked tablecloths with Chianti bottles for candleholders, put up travel posters of Italy, and decorate with long strands of garlic and salami. Cover large serving trays with a mouthwatering array of Italian pasta dishes and antipasto decorated with tiny Italian flag toothpicks. Add the crowning touch by playing Italian music in the background or having a violinist stroll among the tables.

Get into the real spirit and dress the part! You and/or your help can dress appropriately for the theme you've chosen. Clothe yourself in Victorian, Italian, Mexican or Hawaiian attire to become part of the decorating atmosphere. Use things that you have around the house or pick up inexpensive items at local thrift stores. For an elegant cocktail or dinner party, ask the help to dress in black skirts or pants with crisp white shirts.

Keep in mind that decorating is not just balloons and banners, it encompasses everything found at the party. The centerpiece, linens, and dishes you choose are enhanced by the way you fold the napkins and display the food on the buffet table. Whether you place them at each place setting or reserve them for later, your party favors are a not-to-be-forgotten decorating must. The following information is designed to give you ideas so that you can find just the right combination to create that special shower. Feel free to mix and match ideas to get the final look you're after.

Decorating Delights

Balloons — Always fun and festive, these light-hearted charmers can be relied on to create a colorful entrance. You can also attach streamers and let them dangle as the balloons float up to the ceiling. Or use the colorful ties to secure them to the back of each chair, a wine glass or napkin ring.

Banners and Streamers — Printed with congratulations or the couple's names, these are great stretched across an entry way or crisscrossing a room.

Flowers and Plants — Greenery can be just the right touch in creating a simple but striking centerpiece or transforming a room into a lush tropical paradise.

Baby Photos — Enlarge baby pictures of the bride and groom or expectant parents, if it's a baby shower.

Travel Posters — Place travel posters around the room to make your guests feel as if they've arrived at your theme location or the couple's honeymoon destination.

Hats — Mexican sombreros, chefs' hats or vintage Victorian bonnets can be worn or incorporated into distinctive table displays.

If your shower falls near a holiday, you may want to decorate around that holiday theme. Valentine's Day calls for red hearts and white doilies. Easter needs rabbits and chocolate or marshmallow eggs, while Halloween begs for a pumpkin centerpiece. Halloween is also the perfect holiday for caramel and chocolate-covered apples wrapped in cellophane and tied with orange and black curling ribbon. Thanksgiving and Christmas both deserve holiday decorations with chocolate turkeys or glittery Christmas ornaments for party favors.

The Perfect Centerpiece

The centerpiece is deservedly the focal point of the table and as such should coordinate with and complement the rest of the setting. Flowers are by far the most popular choice of centerpieces. Coming in a wide variety of shapes and sizes, floral arrangements are prized for their ability to add the freshness of color to any table setting. Arrange the blossoms you choose loosely in a favorite vase or secure with marbles or rocks. Take care that your arrangement is not distracting to those who will be seated directly in front of it. Flowers should be positioned so that they are either above or below eye level so as not to obstruct some-one's view. As you are adjusting the centerpiece, take the time to step back from the table and look at the bouquet in terms of the overall effect. How high is the ceiling? When it's high, you should opt for a more grandiose spray that can hold its own and not get lost in the room. How wide is the table? You don't want to create an overpowering arrangement.

Small flowers can be artfully grouped in separate glass bowls which, when pushed together, give the illusion of one sweeping arrangement. At the end of the shower give each guest her own bowl of blossoms to take home.

It is easier and more economical to select flowers that are in season. Exotic flowers can be beautiful and expensive so be sure you know the cost before settling on your final arrangement. Keep your color scheme in mind while making your selection and don't be afraid to add a little "spice" to your decorating scheme.

Bouquets can be ordered directly from the florist or you can create them yourself, depending on your budget, time, and talent. When opting to make your own arrangements, be creative in your choice of contain-ers. Your fragrant centerpiece can become delightfully different by being arranged in crystal vases, decorative boxes, ceramic pots, or woven baskets. It's helpful to use a piece of "green oasis" in the bottom of the container so that the flowers have water while being held securely where you place them.

A more casual look for a barbecue with a gardening theme can be achieved by arranging live potted flowers as a centerpiece. You can either paint the pots or cover them in a pretty fabric tied with a bow. Give the pots to the bride at the end of the shower or plant them in your garden as a lovely reminder of a very special day.

An evening affair can be enhanced by a centerpiece which in-corporates votive candles. A mirror can be used as a reflective base on which to set your flowers surrounded by flickering candles. A beautiful alternative is to place slender tapers on either side of the floral display.

When it comes to choosing a centerpiece, don't think just in terms of floral arrangements. There is virtually no limit to the variety of interesting and striking items that can be used to grace the center of your party table.

Just for Variety Centerpieces

Stuffed and ceramic bears — They are cute, fun, and can even be dressed up to suit the occasion!

Dolls — You may want to "invite" a bride doll to your bridal shower or an old fashioned doll to a Victorian tea. And there is always a large assortment of baby dolls ready to come to any baby shower!

Beach Bucket — Fill to overflowing with tropical flowers to add fragrance to your Hawaiian luau or beach party.

Umbrellas — Intertwine pink and white ribbons around the handles of miniature umbrellas to hold fresh flowers in place.

Candles — Select votive, taper, or thick round candles, surrounding the bases with greenery or silk flowers.

Balloons — Attach a helium balloon bouquet to a basket filled with flowers, candy or stuffed animals.

Food — Delight all the senses with an edible centerpiece. A luscious dessert surrounded by colorful blossoms, oversized strawberries piled haphazardly on a silver tray, or a tempting array of fresh fruit carefully arranged in a basket all make a feast for the eyes, as well as the palate.

Chocolate Swans — Let large chocolate swans grace your table. Their hollowed-out backs can be filled with truffles or chocolate-dipped strawberries.

Chocolate Roses — Give into a fabulous spray of chocolate roses, either solo or interspersed with fresh flowers. Present each guest with a long-stemmed delicacy when the celebration is over.

These are just a few ideas that I hope will encourage you to use your imagination when creating your own wonderful centerpiece or adding that very special touch to a scrumptious buffet table. There's very little effort involved and it's well worth the time spent on your own flights of fancy to come up with the touch that is unmistakably "you."

A Beautiful Buffet Table

A buffet table can be a visual treat when the food is well-displayed and tastefully arranged in appropriate serving dishes that are imaginatively garnished. Where the food is placed can either add to or detract from the desired effect. Enhance the theme you've chosen through your selection of linens and serving pieces. If the table is crowded you may have to forego other decorations or reduce the size of your centerpiece.

Since most of the lavish effect of a buffet comes from the food, find creative ways of laying out the feast. Also be sure that you have planned for a sufficient number of serving pieces in the size and type you'll need.

Serving Pieces with Savvy

- Crystal bowls or plates
- Silver trays and platters
- Baskets lined with napkins or scarfs
- Decorative boxes and tins
- Hollowed-out watermelons, pineapples, and oranges
- Champagne or parfait glasses
- Pastry or chocolate shells to be filled
- Hollowed-out cabbages or artichokes for dips
- Chafing dishes to keep food piping hot
- Fondue pots for serving hot meatballs or chocolate for dipping fruits

From Plain to Gorgeous — Making the Food Look Good

After you have gathered all the basics (serving pieces, trays, etc.), it's time to concentrate on the little touches that will give your buffet table pizazz. Doilies, lettuce or kale leaves can be used to line dishes and platters. Sprigs of parsley or mint are meant for those small corners that need a special touch. Lemons, limes, and oranges thinly sliced are perfect for trimming a tray. Also reach for grapes and strawberries, as well as fresh flowers to complete your platters.

Make your food as appealing as possible. Look at the texture and color of the food, as well as how it goes with the other dishes being served. The way you cut or don't cut the food can also add interest and appeal. Vary the size and when looking for a dramatic look, use whole foods — giant strawberries dipped in chocolate are stunning as a dessert. Huge mushrooms stuffed with a tasty filling can be placed side-by-side with whole baby carrots on a tray.

Pay careful attention to the way you arrange the food. Cheese, for example, should be displayed on a cheese board. Place a large uncut portion of the cheese in the back or center and surround with small slices. Use a hollowed-out cabbage or artichoke as a colorful container for dip. Set it in the center of a large tray with cut vegetables encircling it. Arrange food like stuffed snow peas, cookies, or slices of nut bread by overlapping individual pieces in concentric rings.

Table Settings with Style

An empty table comes to life as it is filled with the items you enjoy. Pay close attention to even the smallest detail when creating your table, carefully selecting the right type of table covering, plates, glasses, utensils, and napkins in order to attain the mood you want. Keep in mind that your table should be harmonious. Choose tablecloths that coordinate with your dishes and the style of the party. Achieve a new look by layering different fabrics in either coordinating or contrasting color combinations. Placemats may also be the right choice for the casual table. For an elegant shower, use napkins to create a distinctive place setting. Fold into a fan shape and tuck into a goblet, or simply tie each with an elegant bow. For a slightly less formal look, a large napkin can be tied into a loose knot or dressed up with a napkin ring and placed directly on each plate.

Ideas for Super Settings

Buffet Without Table Seating

- Tray tables should be strategically placed throughout the room to give guests a place to set their drinks.
- Purchase individual wicker lap trays for everyone. They can be decorated and given as party favors or saved for future occasions.
- China, paper, or plastic plates are all appropriate for this type of shower. Plates should be stacked at the beginning of the buffet line.
- When deciding on disposable plates, choose sturdy ones or use wicker plate liners.
- With china, always use stainless or sterling flatware. If you'll be having paper plates, good plastic utensils or your stainless is fine.
- Napkins and flatware should be placed together, either next to the plates or at the end of the buffet. There are a number of ways to arrange the silverware. Choose to line it up neatly or roll each set in a napkin, tie with a bow, and place in a wicker basket or silverware caddy. You can also use a large napkin to tie around each set of utensils, which is then stacked on the table or in a basket.
- Wine, champagne or punch should already be poured and waiting in glasses at the end of the buffet line. If space is at a premium, move the beverages to another area.
- Party favors should be distributed as your guests are leaving.

Buffet with Table Seating

- Count, count, and recount! Make sure that you have an adequate number of tables and chairs, which can be either rented or borrowed.

- Select a colorful tablecloth, whether linen or paper. Linens in a number of lovely shades can be obtained from party rental stores.

- Linen napkins to match or coordinate with the tablecloth are a must for the elegant buffet. For a more casual look, there is a wide selection of paper tablecloths with matching napkins to choose from at your local party supply store. Browse with your budget and style in mind!

- This type of buffet allows the utensils to be positioned next to the plates, at the end of the buffet or in a regular place setting at each table. No matter which you choose, always place the napkin with the silverware.

- Fold each napkin in half and place to the left of each plate with the utensils on top or add the magic of folding it in a special way. What you do with the napkin and where you place it can add life to your table.

- For the casual luncheon with a kitchen theme, turn to scarfs, bandannas, or kitchen towels for napkins and placemats. These eye-catchers can then be taken home by your guests.

- Open seating for this type of party is the easiest but you may want to add a more personal note by using place cards. Choose the style that you feel drawn to.

- An element of surprise adds sparkle so treat your guests to a special party favor at each place setting. Many party favors can double as place cards (SEE PARTY FAVORS.)

- If you are setting the individual tables, set out the wine and water goblets as well. Water glasses should be filled before the guests are seated. An open bottle of wine may be placed at each table for guests to serve themselves. Another option is to fill the wine glasses and place them together either at the end of the buffet line or on a small table.

A Sit-down Meal

- In calculating the seating, don't forget to count yourself and the guest of honor! It's always wise to have a few additional chairs in the event of an additional, last-minute guest.

- Linen tablecloths and napkins should definitely be part of your table on this formal occasion. Although white is always appropriate, you may opt for colored linens to complement your china and decor. With colors in demand, some rental companies now offer printed or the very latest two-tiered tablecloths to choose from. This exciting layered look can be imitated by placing your own square of solid color fabric underneath a shorter coordinated print.

- For this gathering, it's time to bring out your best china, crystal, and silver. If you don't own an elegant service, don't worry, just turn to your local rental company (this may mean dear old Mom.) If you're going to be borrowing the china from several loving relatives, either alternate the different patterns at each place setting or set different tables with their own complete pattern.

- Creating napkins of distinction will turn the ordinary table into a spectacular one. Whether adhering to the simplicity of an elegantly-folded napkin alone or choosing the adornment of a fabulous gold bow, you should choose a napkin that makes a statement. Surprise your guests by using a party favor to embellish each napkin. Purchase a beautiful hair ribbon or lace clip to fasten around each napkin in place of a napkin ring. Your glamorous creations can then be placed to the left of the cutlery or on top of the plates.

- Have your table completely set before the first celebrant arrives. Water glasses are filled just before the guests are seated. Leave guests to serve their own wine from an elegant decanter placed on the table or have a waiter circulate with the wine after all are seated.

Special Party Favors

Although by no means mandatory, party favors are a fun way of remembering an outstanding party. If your budget is quite limited, you may decide not to give party favors or to select those which can double as place cards. If you do decide to give favors, be creative and make them fun!

Fabulous Favors

Potpourri sachet — Available in a wide variety of shapes, sizes, and fabrics, prices are as varied as the selection! You can make your own by cutting 5" squares of fine netting, lace, or fabric and placing a few tablespoons of scented potpourri in the center. Gather the edges and secure with a matching ribbon. These are great for a Victorian tea or lingerie shower.

Chocolate long-stemmed rose — Tie a gold filigree bow around each one, add a card with the name of the guest and voilà! You've just created a place card, too. Or arrange a stunning centerpiece and instruct your guests to each take a rose as they leave.

Chocolate heart or swan — Fill heart-shaped shells or the empty niches in the swans' backs with Jordan almonds or chocolate truffles and then wrap in colored cellophane. Find these delights at gourmet chocolate stores.

Chocolate truffles — Godiva sells small individual gold boxes containing two truffles. Wrap each with a gold ribbon and attach a creamy white place card.

Chocolate mints — Exclusive chocolate stores carry individually-wrapped chocolate mints tied in sets of three. Make your own for less money by purchasing an entire box of mints, dividing into stacks of three, and tying with a narrow pink satin ribbon.

A split of champagne — Wrapped in a shiny swatch of fabric or an elegant napkin and adorned with a silver bow, this serves as the most sophisticated of place cards for the formal, sit-down dinner.

Crystal ring holder — Tie a satin ribbon around the center or fill the base with Jordan almonds and wrap in cellophane.

Silver heart dish — Nestle three truffles in a heart-shaped dish, wrap, and top off with an oversized bow.

Picture frame — Select delicate picture frames to grace each place setting. Write the guest's name on a piece of paper and place it in the window of each frame. A charming place card, it's something everyone can use.

Engraved wine glass — Purchase inexpensive wine glasses and have each one engraved with your guests' names. For a an extra-special effect, tie a helium balloon to the stem and place around the table for each visitor to find.

Porcelain or crystal bells — Bells are a delicate touch for the elegant table. If you want to go all out, a guest's name can be painted or etched on each bell.

Porcelain or fabric-covered boxes — Containers make a favorite catchall to remind everyone of your special shower.

Note paper or thank-you cards — These may be personalized with each guest's initials so that they can also serve as place cards. A pleasing momento, no one can ever have enough!

Jelly Beans or Swedish mints — Buy candies already wrapped in clear boxes or bags. You'll only need to add a bow and you're done!

Bath soaps — Fill a small basket with these scented delights. For a more lavish favor, add fragrant body mousse, bath salts, or a luxurious bath oil.

Teas — Select boxes of gourmet teas, tie individual tea balls to the tops with a pretty ribbon, and you've just completed your Victorian tea decorations!

Refrigerator magnet — Perky and fun, it's the not-so-obvious choice for a kitchen shower.

Christmas ornament — Just the right touch if Christmas is just around the corner.

Baby bears — Everyone loves these little critters. For more elegance, choose those filled with potpourri or dressed in little hats.

Bud vase — For the sit-down luncheon, place a single rose in a bud vase. Affix a place card with a delicate gold ribbon and your table is complete.

Purse size calendar or note pad — Choose a variety of colors so that each guest feels special.

Make-up or lipstick brush — A decorative bow adds a whimsical note to this party favor.

Napkin Folding With Flair

Napkin Roll

1 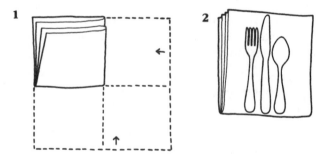 3

1. With right side down, fold into quarters.
2. Place utensils on napkin.
3. Roll napkin around utensils, secure with a ribbon.

The Tulip

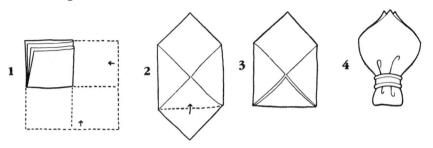

1. With right side down, fold into quarters.
2. Fold left and right corners into center.
3. Fold bottom corner up to center.
4. Turn over with point up, slip on napkin ring.

Fan Fold in Goblet

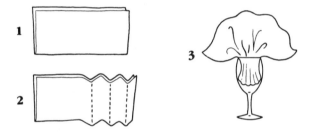

1. Fold napkin in half.
2. Pleat in one-inch accordian pleats from one end to the other.
3. Place one end into a goblet and allow the other to open.

Folded Napkin

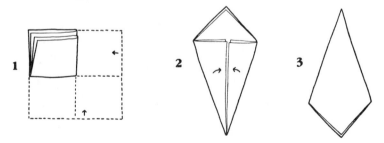

1. With right side down, fold into quarters.
2. Fold left and right corners into center.
3. Turn the napkin over and lay it flat with top pointing up or down.

Fan Fold with Ribbon

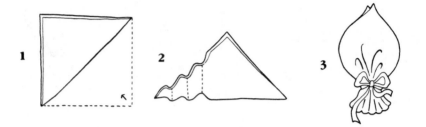

1. Fold napkin in half, diagonally.
2. Pleat in one-inch accordian pleats from one end to the other.
3. Secure with a ribbon a couple of inches up from bottom edge.
4. Lay flat, allowing top to open.

Rolled Napkin

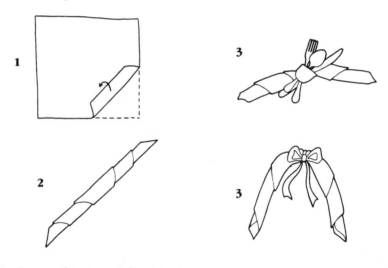

1. Lay napkin out right side down.
2. Roll diagonally from bottom right to upper left.
3. Tie napkin in a knot around utensils; or tie a ribbon around the center of napkin, lay flat in cresent shape.

A
FESTIVE
BRUNCH

Chapter 5

A FESTIVE BRUNCH

Variety is the spice of life and there's no better place to demonstrate this than at an informal brunch. Start your lazy Saturday or Sunday off the right way by beginning your shower at 10:30 or 11:00 AM. Let your guests slowly wake up to a tempting array of tantalizing dishes that can be easily and inexpensively prepared in advance. The number of entrees you decide on is up to you — browse through the following menu and select one or more dishes.

Quiches, Crepes, and Belgian Waffles

MENU

Fresh Fruit Salad

•

Broccoli and Tomato Quiche • Chicken Crepes
Belgian Waffle and Sausage

Assorted Muffins and Coffee Cake

Orange Juice and Champagne • White Wine

Gourmet Coffee and Teas

Fresh Fruit Salad

Create a stunning centerpiece by choosing to serve this refreshing treat in a hollowed-out watermelon or create individual fruit cups by filling empty orange or cantaloup halves. Prepare the salad by slicing, cubing, and scooping out small balls of any combination of the following:

> cantaloup or honeydew melon
> oranges
> tangerines
> bananas
> apples
> pineapple
> strawberries
> grapes

Note: Be sure to dip apples and bananas in lemon juice to prevent them from darkening. To keep these two fruits from becoming mushy, add them to the salad just before serving.

Broccoli and Tomato Quiche

> *1 9" pastry shell, partially baked*
> *5 eggs*
> *1 1/2 cups grated cheese, sharp Cheddar, Monterey Jack or a combination of the two*
> *3/4 pint plain yogurt*
> *1 small head broccoli, broken into florets*
> *1 large tomato, diced*
> *4 green onions, diced*
> *1/4 teaspoon salt*
> *1/8 teaspoon pepper*

In a large bowl, beat eggs and yogurt together. Mix in salt and pepper and set aside. Sprinkle half of the grated cheese over the bottom of the pastry shell. Arrange the broccoli over the cheese, distributing evenly. Spread the green onions and diced tomatoes over the broccoli, cover with the remaining cheese. Pour the egg and yogurt mixture over all. Bake at 375° for 40-45 minutes or until the center is solid.

Chicken Crepes

> *12-16 crepes*
> *5 tablespoons butter or margarine*
> *1 small onion, chopped*
> *1/4 pound mushrooms, sliced*
> *3 tablespoons all-purpose flour*
> *2/3 cups chicken broth*
> *1/2 cup half-and-half (light cream)*

1 (8 ounce) can artichoke hearts
2 cups cooked chicken, diced
1/3 cup grated Parmesan cheese
1/4 teaspoon rosemary
1/2 Swiss cheese, shredded
1/2 teaspoon salt

In a frying pan over medium heat, melt 2 tablespoons butter. Add onions and mushrooms and cook until limp. Stir in remaining butter. When melted, slowly blend in flour. Gradually add the broth and half-and-half. Cook until the mixture comes to a boil and thickens. Remove from heat. Cut artichokes in thirds and add to sauce along with chicken, Parmesan cheese, rosemary, and salt. Let mixture cool. Divide the filling evenly among the crepes, spooning the mixture into the center of each and folding to close. Crepes can be made to this point and frozen.

To bake, arrange desired number of crepes in a lightly greased shallow casserole dish. Cover and bake at 375° for 20 minutes (35-40 minutes if frozen.) Remove cover and sprinkle 1 tablespoon Swiss cheese over each crepe. Return casserole to the oven just until the cheese melts.

MAKES 6-8 SERVINGS OF 2 CREPES EACH

Crepes:

1 cup milk
3 eggs
2/3 cup all-purpose flour
4 teaspoons butter or margarine

Blend milk and eggs, whisking in flour until smooth. Let set at room temperature for one hour. Place a 6 or 7" crepe or frying pan on the stove over medium heat. When hot, coat the bottom of the pan with 1/4 teaspoon butter. Stir batter and ladle in 2 tablespoons, quickly tilting the pan back and forth so that the entire surface is covered. If the pan is hot enough, the crepe should quickly set and begin to form tiny bubbles. Continue cooking until the surface is dry and the edges lightly browned. Flip with a spatula and brown the other side. Turn the crepe out onto a platter and start the next crepe. Place wax paper between the crepes as you layer them so that they can be easily separated. Crepes can be refrigerated in airtight plastic baggies for up to one week or frozen for as long as six weeks. Allow the crepes to come to room temperature before separating.

MAKES 12-16 CREPES

Belgian Waffles

> *4 eggs, separated*
> *2 tablespoons granulated sugar*
> *1/2 teaspoon salt*
> *1 cup milk*
> *1/2 teaspoon vanilla*
> *4 tablespoons butter or margarine, melted and cooled*
> *1 cup all-purpose flour*
> *melted butter or margarine*
> *powdered sugar*
> *sweetened whipped cream*
> *strawberries, whole or sliced*

In a medium bowl, beat egg whites just until stiff, set aside. In a large bowl, combine egg yolks, sugar, and salt, and beat until thick. Blend in milk, vanilla, and 4 tablespoons butter. While continuing to beat, add flour and blend well. Gently fold in egg whites.

Preheat Belgian waffle iron according to manufacturer's directions and brush with butter if required. Pour recommended amount of batter onto waffle iron, spreading evenly to cover grids. Bake according to printed instructions. To serve, let waffle cool slightly and dust with powdered sugar before topping with whipped cream and strawberries. Serve with cooked sausage links or bacon on the side. To keep the buffet line moving, borrow an additional iron from a friend and have a helper start making waffles before the guests sit down.

MAKES 5 WAFFLES

An Omelette Party

Omelettes are wonderfully suited to parties of all sizes. Even though everything appears to happen all at once, the ingredients can be chopped and prepared in advance, leaving just the brief cooking until the last minute. A boon to those watching their budget, fillings for omelettes are inexpensive and readily available. The actual cooking can become entertainment in itself and lends a nice bit of action to your buffet table. In order to highlight your brunch delicacies, choose to cook the omelettes on a center island cook top. If your kitchen is arranged differently, rent a two-burner tabletop stove unit and place it on the table with the fillings within easy reach. For cooking ease, have each filling ingredient in its own separate bowl. Although, with a good pan at a high temperature, omelettes cook rapidly, you may want to have a second pan going at the same time. Get your best friend who loves to cook to help with that extra pan.

Melon Wedges Wrapped in Prosciutto

1/2 pound prosciutto ham, thinly sliced
2 melons

The flavor of prosciutto, a cured ham from Italy, is a true delicacy but if you just can't find it, choose thinly-sliced ham or turkey ham instead. Divide each slice in half lengthwise. Cut melon in half and scoop out the seeds. Quarter each piece, then slice into eighths. With a sharp paring knife, remove the rind from each wedge. Wrap one slice of ham around each wedge and secure by overlapping the edges.

Individual Omelettes

Once you have a little practice, you'll be able to turn out an omelette in about one minute. You will need an omelette or 7-8" heavy frying pan with sloping sides. Allow 2-3 eggs for each omelette and select appropriate fillings from those listed below.

The Omelette

2-3 eggs
1 tablespoon water
1 tablespoon melted butter
salt and pepper to taste

Beat eggs well and add salt, pepper, and water. In the meantime, heat the omelette pan over medium high heat. Add melted butter and tilt pan to coat bottom and sides. Heat until hot but not smoking, pour in egg mixture and cook. As omelette begins to set, gently lift sides to allow uncooked mixture from top to flow underneath the omelette. Move pan continuously to prevent sticking and continue cooking until the liquid is gone but the top is still moist and creamy. Spoon 3-4 table-

51

spoons of filling into the center and distribute evenly down the middle of the omelette. Fold the omelette in half and gently slide out onto serving plate.

Fantastic Fillings (Choose your own special combinations):

shredded Cheddar and Swiss cheese
sliced mushrooms sauteed in butter and sherry
diced salami or ham
diced tomatoes
diced avocado
thinly-sliced spinach leaves
asparagus tips, lightly steamed
bacon bits
baby shrimp
sour cream
hot salsa
jalapeno peppers
smoked salmon
whipped cream cheese
green peppers
black olives

Muffins, Biscuits, and Coffee Cake

Let the tantalizing aroma of freshly-baked goods complement your brunch. Present these delicious crowd-pleasers on a tray or piled in a basket. Purchased croissants or bagels should come from a bakery specializing in these delicacies to insure their freshness.

Apple Muffins

1 egg, beaten
1 cup milk
4 tablespoons vegetable oil
2 cups sifted flour
4 teaspoons baking powder
1/2 teaspoon salt
2 tablespoons sugar
1 cup sweetened applesauce

Combine egg with milk and vegetable oil. Sift flour together with baking powder, salt, and sugar. Stir lightly into milk and egg mixture, mixing only until flour is dampened. Using a greased muffin tin, drop just enough batter into each cup to cover the bottom. Spread a rounded teaspoon of applesauce over batter and fill sections 3/4's full with remaining batter. Bake at 375° for approximately 25 minutes or until toothpick inserted comes out dry.

MAKES 12 SMALL OR 6 LARGE MUFFINS

Blueberry Crumb Muffins

1/4 cup shortening
1/4 cup sugar
1 egg, well beaten
1 cup sifted flour
3 teaspoons baking powder
1/2 teaspoon salt
1 cup fine dry bread crumbs
1 cup milk
1 cup fresh blueberries (substitute frozen if needed)

Cream the shortening and sugar together until light. Stir in the well-beaten egg. Sift together flour, baking powder, and salt, and add bread crumbs. Combine crumbs with the creamed mixture by thirds, alternating with milk. Lightly stir in the blueberries being careful not to crush them. Ladle into well-greased muffin pans, filling them about 2/3's full. Bake at 375° for 25 minutes, testing with a toothpick to check if baked.

MAKES 12 MEDIUM-SIZED MUFFINS

Buttermilk Biscuits

2 cups sifted flour
1 teaspoon salt
2 teaspoons baking powder
1/4 teaspoon baking soda
1/3 cup solid vegetable shortening
3/4 cup cold buttermilk
1/4 cup heavy cream (optional glaze)

Preheat oven to 450°. In a large bowl, sift dry ingredients together and cut in shortening until texture resembles coarse oats. Form a well in the center and pour in buttermilk, stir quickly with a fork just to mix. On a lightly floured board, knead mixture eight times, then roll out dough to 1/2" thickness. Cut in rounds with a floured biscuit cutter or rim of a drinking glass. Gather scraps together, roll, and cut remaining dough until all is used.

Place on ungreased baking sheets about 1" apart. Brush with heavy cream and bake 12-15 minutes until golden brown.

MAKES 16-20 BISCUITS

Pecan Sour Cream Coffee Cake

1/2 cup butter or margarine
1 cup granulated sugar
3 eggs
2 cups sifted flour
1 teaspoon baking powder
1 teaspoon baking soda
1/4 teaspoon salt
1 cup sour cream
1/2 cup raisins

Pecan Topping:

3/4 cup brown sugar, firmly packed
1 tablespoon flour
1 teaspoon cinnamon
2 tablespoons butter or margarine
1 cup chopped pecans

To make topping, combine brown sugar, flour, and cinnamon, and mix thoroughly. Cut in butter until the consistency of cornmeal, mix in pecans and set aside. In a large mixing bowl, cream together butter and sugar. Add eggs one at a time, beating after each addition. Sift together flour, baking powder, baking soda, and salt. Add to creamed mixture alternating with sour cream, blending well after each addition. Stir in raisins.

Spread mixture in a greased 9 x 13 x 2" pan and sprinkle with topping. Bake at 350° (325° for glass) for 30 minutes until it tests done. Cut into squares and serve warm or cold.

SERVES 12

Sticky Buns

1 package active dry yeast
1/4 cup sugar
1 teaspoon salt
1/4 teaspoon soda
2 1/2 - 3 cups flour
1 cup buttermilk
3 tablespoons salad oil
2 tablespoons water
4 tablespoons melted butter
1/2 cup brown sugar, firmly packed
3/4 cup pecan pieces
1 teaspoon cinnamon

In a large bowl, combine 1 cup flour, sugar, salt, soda, and yeast. Warm buttermilk and oil over medium heat, add to dry mixture and beat. Gradually stir in the remaining 1 1/2 cups of flour while continuing to beat. Turn out onto a floured board and knead dough until smooth and elastic, adding more flour if dough is too sticky. Set aside.

Prepare topping by combining 2 tablespoons of melted butter, 2 tablespoons water, and 1/4 cup brown sugar. Divide topping equally and sprinkle into twelve 2 1/2" muffin tins, covering with pecan pieces.

Roll out dough into 12 x 15" rectangle. Brush surface with the remaining 2 tablespoons butter. Blend cinnamon and the rest of the brown sugar together and sprinkle evenly over buttered dough. Beginning from the narrow end, roll dough lengthwise into a cylinder. Cut 12 1" slices and place each, cut side down, into a muffin cup. Let rise until double in bulk, about 1 1/2 hours. Bake at 350° for 25 minutes, until golden brown. Turn out onto flat serving plate, leaving muffin tin briefly on top of rolls to allow topping to drizzle over buns. Cool before serving.

MAKES 12 BUNS

A
SUMPTUOUS
LUNCHEON

Chapter 6

A SUMPTUOUS LUNCHEON

Whether sit-down or buffet, a luncheon is a festive affair characterized by light, elegantly prepared dishes enhanced by a generous assortment of breads, croissants, rolls, and muffins. The meal centers around a light main course, such as poached fish or a delicate chicken dish, and may be composed of three or four courses. When planning your menu, try to take advantage of recipes which allow dishes to be prepared well in advance and reheated or served cold.

Formal Luncheon

MENU

Mushrooms Florentine

Lemon Sherbert

Chicken Salad in Artichokes

Croissants and Sweet Butter

Double Chocolate Torte with Chantilly Cream

Champagne   *White Wine*

Espresso   *Cafe au Lait*   *Tea*

Mushrooms Florentine

12 large mushrooms (2 1/2-3" in diameter)
2 pounds fresh spinach or 1 (10 ounce) package frozen spinach
3 tablespoons butter
1 medium onion, minced
1 egg yolk
1/2 teaspoon salt
1/8 teaspoon pepper
1/8 teaspoon ground nutmeg (fresh, if possible)
1/4 cup grated Parmesan cheese

Preheat oven to 325°. Clean mushrooms and snap out stems. Finely chop stems and set aside. Thoroughly wash and drain spinach leaves. Cook, covered, using only the water that clings to the leaves, for 4-5 minutes. Squeeze out all the water from the spinach and chop finely. If using frozen spinach, be sure to drain excess water very well.

Place mushroom caps into a 8 x 12" baking dish. Melt butter over medium heat, add onion and mushroom stems and saute until onion is translucent. Stir in the spinach and remove pan from heat.

Combine the egg yolk, salt, pepper, nutmeg, 2 1/2 tablespoons of Parmesan cheese and add to the spinach mixture. Stuff each individual mushroom cap with mix and sprinkle with remaining cheese. If made ahead, cover with plastic wrap and refrigerate up to 24 hours.

Bake, uncovered, for 20 minutes or until heated through and tender. Allot one or two mushrooms per person.

Iced Lemon Sherbert

To cleanse the palate between courses, serve a small scoop of lemon sherbert in a liqueur or small wine glass. Garnish with a sprig of fresh mint.

Chicken Salad in Artichokes

6 large chicken breasts, halved
2 cups mayonnaise
2 (6 ounce) jars artichoke hearts
2 teaspoons pressed or minced garlic
1 (8 ounce) can hearts of palm, drained and sliced
white wine for poaching
5-6 cooked artichokes, chilled and hollowed out (optional)

Drain marinated artichoke hearts, reserving oil. Slice hearts in half and set aside. In a small bowl, combine the artichoke marinade, garlic, and mayonnaise and place in the refrigerator.

In a saucepan, poach chicken breasts in enough white wine to cover. Bring to a boil, immediately reduce heat, and simmer uncovered for about 14 minutes or until done. Remove, drain, and allow to cool to room temperature. Remove skin, debone, and cut chicken into bite-sized pieces.

Toss chicken, hearts of palm, and artichoke slices with mayonnaise mixture thoroughly to coat. Mixture may be stored one day. Serve mounded in hollowed-out artichoke shells or on a bed of lettuce.

SERVES 5-6

Double Chocolate Torte

9 ounces bittersweet chocolate
6 ounces sweet butter
6 eggs, separated
1 cup granulated sugar
1/4 cup flour
1/4 teaspoon salt
2 tablespoons confectioner's sugar
1 cup Chantilly cream

Preheat oven to 325°. Break chocolate into small pieces and melt with the butter in a bowl over simmering water. Whip the egg yolks with 3/4 cup of the granulated sugar. Gradually mix in flour, then add the melted chocolate and butter and blend well.

In a separate bowl, whip the egg whites, salt, and remaining granulated sugar to soft peaks, then fold gently into chocolate mixture.

Butter a 9" round cake pan and dust with flour. Pour the batter into the pan. Bake 30-40 minutes, until the center of the cake is still moist but no longer runny. Cool and turn out onto a platter.

To serve, dust the top with confectioner's sugar. Slice cake thinly and add a dollop of Chantilly cream.

Chantilly cream:

1 cup heavy cream, chilled
1 1/2 teaspoons fine sugar
1/2 teaspoon vanilla extract
pinch of salt

Mix all the ingredients together and whip to soft peaks. Chill thoroughly.

YIELDS 1 1/2 CUPS

A Beautiful Buffet

A good buffet depends on variety. As you plan your menu, remember to offer a bountiful selection of salads to complement one special entree. Select dishes in an assortment of textures and colors so that your table is a feast for the eyes, as well as the palate.

MENU

Tossed Green Salad   Marinated Pasta Salad

Carrot Pineapple Toss   Waldorf Salad

Honey Dijon Chicken

Croissants and Sweet Butter

Apricot Upside-down Cake

White Wine   Gourmet Coffee   Tea

Marinated Pasta Salad

> 1 pound corkscrew pasta, all white or a mixture of wheat, spinach
> and tomato pastas
> 3/4 cup olive oil
> 4 green olives, thinly sliced
> 1 red pepper, finely chopped
> 2 large carrots, shredded coarsely
> 3 yellow squash, coarsely chopped
> 1 pound fresh broccoli, lightly streamed until just tender
> 2 tablespoons chives, minced
> 1 cup fresh basil, chopped
> 1 cup Parmesan cheese, freshly grated
> 1 tablespoon Dijon mustard
> 1/4 cup balsamic vinegar
> 3 garlic cloves, minced
> 1 teaspoon sugar
> red pepper flakes, crushed
> black pepper
> salt

Cook pasta in boiling water al dente (firm.) Drain and immediately toss with 1/4 cup olive oil and cool to room temperature, stirring occasionally. Add green onions, red peppers, carrots, squash, broccoli, chives, chopped basil, and 3/4 cup Parmesan cheese. Mix thoroughly, using hands.

Blend together mustard, vinegar, garlic, sugar, salt, and pepper, adding red pepper flakes to taste. While beating continuously, slowly add remaining olive oil. Pour over pasta and toss to mix well. Refrigerate if dish is being prepared for following day. Allow pasta to sit at room temperature for at least 2 hours before serving. Sprinkle with Parmesan cheese immediately before bringing to the table.

SERVES 12

Carrot Pineapple Toss

4 large carrots, peeled and shredded
1 cup raisins, soaked in 2 cups water until plump
1 cup canned pineapple chunks, drained
1/2 cup mayonnaise

Place shredded carrots, raisins, and pineapple in a large bowl. Add mayonnaise and toss to thoroughly coat. Cover and chill until ready to serve.

SERVES 6-8

Waldorf Salad

6 medium red apples, cored and diced (do not peel)
1 cup celery, finely chopped
1/2 cup walnuts, coarsely chopped
2/3-1 cup mayonnaise

In a large bowl, stir all ingredients together, adding just enough mayonnaise to ensure creamy consistency. Cover and chill 2-3 hours.

SERVES 16-18

Honey Dijon Chicken

8 chicken breasts, skinned, boned, and sliced in half
8 tablespoons Dijon mustard
4 tablespoons honey
2 tablespoons fresh lemon juice

In a small, bowl mix mustard, honey, and lemon juice and blend well. Place chicken breasts in a shallow baking dish and cover with sauce. Baked, uncovered, at 350° for approximately 20 minutes, until chicken is cooked through but still moist.

SERVES 16

Apricot Upside-down Cake

4-6 tablespoons butter
3/4 cup brown sugar, firmly packed
2 (8 ounce) cans pitted apricot halves in syrup
1 cup all-purpose flour
1 teaspoon baking powder
1/4 teaspoon salt
3 eggs
1 cup granulated sugar
1/2 gallon French vanilla ice cream

In a heavy 10" frying pan with an ovenproof handle, melt butter over medium heat. Add brown sugar and cook, stirring constantly, for about 10 minutes, being careful that it doesn't burn. Drain apricots and reserve 1/4 cup of the syrup. Place apricot halves, cut side up, in a single layer as close as possible to each other over brown sugar in skillet; set aside to cool.

In a small bowl, combine flour, baking powder, and salt; set aside. In another bowl, beat eggs with granulated sugar until light and fluffy, stir in 1/4 cup syrup. Gently fold dry ingredients into egg mixture and pour over apricots. Bake uncovered at 350° for 35-40 minutes until tooth pick inserted comes out clean. Immediately loosen cake with a spatula and invert onto serving platter.

Let skillet rest briefly on inverted cake to allow syrup to drizzle over cake. Serve warm with French vanilla ice cream. If cooked ahead of time, warm briefly in microwave or oven.

SERVES 8

A
VICTORIAN
TEA

Chapter 7

A VICTORIAN TEA

Reminiscent of a less harried era, the Victorian tea is a luxurious way to pass an afternoon in celebration with special people. Whether you own, rent, or borrow the items you'll need, this is the perfect showcase for the finest linens, china, and silver. You'll find it a pleasure to be the hostess of a unique shower that gently speaks of elegance and cherished friendships.

MENU

Assorted Tea Sandwiches

Orange Scones

Madeleines　　*Russian Tea cakes*　　*Linzer Hearts*

Bundt Cake　　*Victorian Walnut Bread*

Shortbread Cookies　　*Personalized Initial Cookies*

Punch　　*Tea*

Assorted Tea Sandwiches

Purchase thinly-sliced loaves of firm white, wheat, and pumpernickel bread from a good bakery. Use a sharp knife to remove crusts, then cut the slices into assorted rectangles, triangles, and circles. Cover with plastic wrap, removing only the piece of bread you are working with. Lightly spread one side of the bread with butter or mayonnaise. Top with various fillings for open-faced sandwiches. For regular sandwiches, spread a thin layer of filling between two buttered slices of bread.

For variety, create a two-toned, layered sandwich by alternating two pieces of white with two pieces of wheat bread separated by a thin layer of cream cheese.

Fine Fillings:

> smoked turkey with cranberry sauce
> cream cheese with walnuts
> steamed baby shrimp on watercress
> chicken salad
> avocado and diced olives
> tuna sprinkled with dill
> sliced hard-boiled egg and cucumber

Breads, Cookies, and Pastries

Orange Scones

> *3 cups flour (adjust as needed)*
> *2/3 cup brown sugar*
> *1 teaspoon baking soda*
> *1 tablespoon grated orange peel*
> *1/2 cup butter (do not soften)*
> *3/4 cup currants*
> *3/4 cup buttermilk*

Mix flour, sugar, baking soda, baking powder, and orange peel in a large mixing bowl. Using a pastry cutter or two knives, cut in butter until the consistency of crumbs. Add currants and buttermilk and mix until evenly moistened. Turn out on lightly-floured board and knead for 10 minutes, until smooth and elastic. Flatten into 1" thick circle and use cookie cutter to cut out 3" circles. Bake in preheated 400° oven 15-20 minutes, until golden. Cool on wire rack. Best served still warm from the oven!

Madeleines

These little cakes are baked in small individual molds with fluted bottoms. You will need two madeleine sets, each containing a dozen individual molds.

> *2 tablespoons clarified butter*
> *1/2 cup sifted cake flour*
> *1/8 teaspoon salt*
> *2 eggs*
> *1/3 cup sugar*

1/2 teaspoon lemon rind, finely grated
1/4 cup butter, melted
confectioner's sugar

Preheat oven to 350°. Brush molds with clarified butter and refrigerate until needed. Sift flour and salt together. In a separate bowl, beat eggs until frothy, add sugar two tablespoons at a time, beating well after each addition. Continue beating at high speed until very thick and lemon colored. Fold in flour 1/3 at a time. Blend lemon rind and butter and fold into batter, one tablespoon at a time.

Fill each mold 2/3's full. Place on baking sheets and bake 14-16 minutes, until golden brown and tops spring back when lightly touched. Cool in molds 1-2 minutes, invert fluted side up onto wire racks to continue cooling. Dust with confectioner's sugar and serve.

MAKES 24

Russian Tea Cakes

1 cup butter, softened
1/2 cup confectioner's sugar
1 teaspoon vanilla
2 1/4 cups sifted flour
1/4 teaspoon salt
3/4 cup nuts, finely chopped

Preheat oven to 400°. Mix butter, sugar and vanilla, blending well. Sift together flour and salt, and add nuts. Work into nut mixture. Shape dough into 1" balls and place on an ungreased cookie sheet.

Bake 10-12 minutes until set but not brown. While still warm, roll in confectioner's sugar. Cool and roll in sugar once more.

MAKES 4 DOZEN

Linzer Hearts

3/4 pound sweet butter, softened
1 3/4 cups confectioner's sugar
1 egg
2 cups all-purpose flour, sifted
1 cup cornstarch
2 cups shelled walnuts, finely ground
1/2 cup red raspberry preserves

Cream butter and 1 cup sugar until light and fluffy. Add egg and mix well. Sift together the flour and cornstarch, add to creamed mixture and blend. Stir in walnuts. Gather dough into a ball, wrap in waxed paper, and chill for 4-6 hours. Roll out to 1/4" thickness. Using a small, heart-shaped cookie cutter, cut out cookies and place on an ungreased cookie sheet. Chill for 45 minutes.

69

Preheat oven to 325°. Bake cookies for 10-15 minutes, until evenly and lightly browned. Remove to rack to cool. While they are still slightly warm, spread half of the cookies with the preserves, using 1/4 teaspoon for each. Use the remaining cookies to place on top of the jam-covered bottoms. Sift remaining confectioner's sugar into a bowl and dip tops and bottoms of cookies to coat.

MAKES 4 DOZEN

Bundt Cake

1 1/2 sticks sweet butter, softened
1 1/2 cups sugar
5 eggs
1 cup sour cream
1 teaspoon vanilla
2 teaspoons baking powder
1 teaspoon baking soda
1/2 teaspoon salt
3 cups flour, sifted

Streusel:

1/2 cup sugar
1 ounce unsweetened chocolate or cocoa
1 teaspoon ground cinnamon
3/4 cup nuts, finely chopped

Preheat oven to 350°. Cream together butter and sugar until fluffy. Add eggs, one at a time, beating well after each. Stir in sour cream and vanilla. In a separate bowl, sift together the dry ingredients. Gradually stir into the batter, blending well.

In another bowl, prepare streusel by combining all ingredients.

Grease and flour a 10" Bundt pan. Pour in half the batter, sprinkle with half of the streusel mixture, and top with remaining batter. Dust the top with the rest of the streusel. Bake for 50-55 minutes, until it tests done with a toothpick.

Victorian Walnut Bread

2 1/2 cups flour, sifted
1 cup sugar
3 1/2 teaspoons baking powder
1 teaspoon salt
3 tablespoons vegetable oil
1 1/4 cups milk
1 egg
1 cup walnuts, finely chopped

Grease and flour one 9 x 5 x 3" loaf pan or two 8 1/2" x 4 1/2" x 2 1/2" loaf pans. In a large bowl, add all ingredients and beat until thoroughly mixed. Pour into prepared pans and bake in preheated 350° oven for 55-65 minutes. Remove from pan and cool before slicing.

Variation:
Add one cup finely chopped dates to batter.

Shortbread Cookies

> *3/4 pound sweet butter, softened*
> *1 cup confectioner's sugar*
> *3 cups all-purpose flour, sifted*
> *1/2 teaspoon salt*
> *1/2 teaspoon vanilla extract*
> *1/4 cup granulated sugar*

Cream butter and confectioner's sugar together until light. Sift flour and salt together and add to mixture. Blend in vanilla. Form dough into ball, wrap in waxed paper, and chill for 4-6 hours. Roll out to 5/8" thickness. Using a 3" cookie cutter, cut out cookies. Sprinkle with granulated sugar and place on ungreased cookie sheets. Refrigerate for 45 minutes.

Bake in preheated oven at 325° for 20 minutes or until just starting to color lightly; cookies should not brown at all. Cool completely on a wire rack.

MAKES 20 COOKIES

Personalized Initial Cookies

> *1 cup butter, softened*
> *1/2 teaspoon salt*
> *1 cup sifted flour*
> *1/2 teaspoon grated lemon rind*
> *1 1/2 tablespoons lemon juice*
> *8 egg yolks*
> *4 cups flour, sifted*

Beat together butter and salt. Add 1 cup sugar gradually and blend until creamy. Mix in grated lemon rind and lemon juice. Beat in the egg yolks, then slowly blend in the remaining 4 cups of flour and chill one hour. Roll the dough into sticks 1/4" in diameter and shape into alphabet letters. Brush lightly with egg yolk and sprinkle with colored or white sugar. Bake on ungreased cookie sheet in preheated 375° oven for 6-8 minutes.

Champagne Punch

> *1 gallon Sauterne wine*
> *4 bottles champagne, one quart each*
> *2 bottles ginger ale, one quart each*
> *1/2 pint sherbert*

Chill wine, champagne, and ginger ale. Pour into large punch bowl, add sherbert and ice cubes just before serving.

SERVES 40

Ladies Punch (Non-alcoholic)

> *2 cans frozen orange juice*
> *2 cans frozen lemonade*
> *8 cans of cold water*
> *2 cups Grenadine*
> *Juice of three fresh lemons*
> *3 quarts ginger ale, chilled*

Mix all together in a large punch bowl right before serving. Float orange slices and cherries on the top and add ice cubes.

SERVES 20

Brewing The Perfect Cup of Tea

Set up a small table or serving trolley with a pot of steaming hot water, a full pot of freshly made tea, a cream pitcher with milk or cream, a sugar bowl filled with sugar cubes, a pair of tongs or small spoon for the sugar cubes, and a small plate of lemon circles or wedges. For an extra special touch, offer a small plate filled with clove-studded lemon wedges to float in each tea cup.

Bring a pot of fresh water to a boil but do not let it continue to boil; overboiling creates a tea with a flat, muddy taste. Pack a tea ball with choice tea, leaving enough space for the leaves to expand slightly when wet. Rinse out the teapot with a small amount of hot water to warm it. Pour in the fresh, hot water, add the tea ball, and let steep for five minutes, long enough to allow the true flavor to "blossom." Stir and remove the tea ball (or bags, if you have used them.) If you have made the tea with loose tea leaves, be sure to place a strainer over the tea cups as you pour to catch any escaping leaves.

There are numerous, mouth-watering teas on the market, select your favorite. Darjeeling, Orange Pekoe, and Earl Gray are just a few of the reliable and wonderful favorites for afternoon tea. In figuring out how much tea to use in the pot, count one teaspoon for each cup of tea and add an extra teaspoon "for the pot." Relax and enjoy!

A
DESSERT
PARTY

Chapter 8

A DESSERT PARTY

When it comes to desserts, there's no such thing as too many, so go ahead and plan a party that will be sweetly sensational! Centering your shower around these luscious treats allows you to spoil your guests by combining two not-to-be-missed luxuries — good friends and sweet desserts.

Menu

Blueberry Cream Cheese Tart   *Apricot Upside-down Cake*

Chocolate Coconut Bars

Double Chocolate Torte   *Chocolate Whiskey Cake*

Cherry Cheesecake   *Amaretto Mousse*

Fresh Strawberries Dipped in Chocolate

Champagne

Cafe Especial

Blueberry Cream Cheese Tart

4 ounces natural cream cheese
1/4 cup sour cream
1-2 teaspoons sugar
3 cups blueberries1/4 cup sugar
nutmeg
grated peel of one lemon
powdered sugar
tart dough

Tart Dough:

1 cup all-purpose flour
pinch salt
1 tablespoon sugar
1/4 teaspoon grated orange peel
4 ounces unsalted butter, room temperature
1 tablespoon water
1/2 teaspoon vanilla

Combine the flour, salt, sugar, and orange peel in a bowl. Cut the butter into small pieces, then cut in dry ingredients, using two knives or a pastry cutter, to make a coarse meal. Combine water and vanilla and stir into mixture with a fork. Gather dough into a ball and flatten into a round disc, wrap in plastic, and place in the refrigerator for 1/2 hour.

Line a 9" tart pan with dough, shaping the sides first. Using your hands, shape sides of uniform thickness, forming an edge that rises about 1/4" above the rim of the pan. Press dough gently into bottom of pan and place in freezer for 30 minutes. Prink bottom of tart with a fork and bake at 400° for 15 minutes until golden brown. Set aside to cool.

Cream Cheese Filling:

Beat together the cream cheese, sour cream, and lemon until they are well combined. Add 1-2 teaspoons sugar and a pinch of nutmeg.

Heat 1/2 cup berries in a saucepan. As soon as they begin to release their juices, add 1/4 cup sugar and continue cooking until smooth and syrupy (about 1-2 minutes.) Pour cooked fruit over rest of berries and gently mix.

To assemble, spread cream cheese mixture evenly over crust and top with berries. Dust edges with powdered sugar. Remove tart carefully from its ring and set on a flat serving plate. Cut into wedges for serving.

SERVES 6-8

Apricot Upside-down Cake
(SEE PAGE 64)

Chocolate Coconut Bars

>   1/2 cup butter
>   1 1/2 cups graham cracker crumbs
>   1 (14 ounce) can sweetened condensed milk (not evaporated milk)
>   1 (6 ounce) package semi-sweet chocolate chips
>   1 cup walnuts, chopped
>   1 (3 1/2 ounce) can flaked coconut

Preheat oven to 350° (325° for glass dish.) Melt butter in a 13 x 9" baking pan by placing briefly in oven. Sprinkle crumbs over butter, mix, and press firmly into bottom of pan. Pour condensed milk evenly over crumbs and top with chocolate chips, walnuts, and flaked coconut; press down firmly.

Bake 25-30 minutes or until lightly browned. Cool thoroughly before cutting.

MAKES 24 BARS

Double Chocolate Torte
(SEE PAGE 61)

Chocolate Whiskey Cake

>   1/2 cup seedless raisins
>   2/3 cup bourbon whiskey
>   1 cup sugar
>   1/4 cup water
>   10 ounces unsweetened chocolate, cut in pieces
>   3/4 cup butter
>   6 eggs, separated
>   1 cup blanched almonds, ground
>   1/2 cup flour

Soak raisins in whiskey. Bring sugar and water to a boil, add chocolate and remove from heat, stirring to melt. Set aside to cool. With electric mixer, beat butter until softened. Beat in egg yolks one at a time. With mixer on low speed, beat in half the chocolate mixture followed by half the ground almonds. Repeat with remaining mixtures. Add whiskey and raisins, beat in flour. Beat egg whites until stiff and fold into batter. Line bottom of 9" tube springform pan with wax paper, grease, and flour. Bake in 375° oven for 30 minutes. Garnish with sliced almonds and dust liberally with powdered sugar.

Cherry Cheesecake

Crust:

>   1 1/2 cups graham cracker crumbs
>   1/4 cup sugar
>   5 tablespoons melted butter

Filling:

>   2 (8 ounce) packages cream cheese, softened
>   2 eggs
>   1/2 cup sugar
>   1 teaspoon vanilla

Cheesecake Topping:

>   1 cup sour cream
>   1/4 cup sugar
>   1 teaspoon vanilla

Preheat oven to 375°. Mix crust ingredients and press firmly into bottom of 9" springform pan, pressing mixture 1/3 of the way up the sides. Beat filling ingredients with electric mixer until satiny and pour into crust. Bake 20 minutes, remove and cool 15 minutes. Increase oven temperature to 475°. Blend topping ingredients together and spread over cooled filling. Return cake to oven and bake 10 minutes longer. Cool to room temperature in pan.

Prepare cherry topping by mixing sugar and cornstarch in a pan. Gradually blend in cherry juice mixture and heat, stirring, until it comes to a boil. Reduce heat and simmer 5 minutes, stirring occasionally. Remove from heat and mix in lemon juice, cherries, and food coloring. Cool 5 minutes. Spread cheesecake with cherry topping and refrigerate 10-12 hours before serving.

Cherry Topping:

>   1/2 cup sugar
>   2 tablespoons cornstarch
>   1 (16 ounce) can sour red cherries, drained (reserve liquid)
>   juice from cherries plus enough water to equal 3/4 cup liquid
>   few drops red food coloring

SERVES 10

Amaretto Mousse

4 tablespoons sweet butter
5 eggs
1 cup granulated sugar
1 1/2 teaspoons unflavored gelatin
3/4 cup tiny macaroons (amaretti), crushed
1 1/2 tablespoons Amaretto liqueur
1 1/2 cups heavy cream, chilled

Melt butter in top half of a double boiler over simmering water. Beat eggs with sugar; add gelatin. Stir into melted butter and cook, stirring continuously, until thickened (6-8 minutes.) Remove from heat. Mix in the Amaretto and crushed macaroons, blending thoroughly. Cool and place in refrigerator until mixture just begins to set.

Whip cream to soft peaks and gently fold into Amaretto mixture. Spoon into individual wine goblets or a large glass serving bowl. Chill until set, approximately 4 hours. Sprinkle with crushed macaroons and serve.

SERVES 8-10

Fresh Strawberries Dipped in Chocolate

Fresh strawberries, rinsed with stems left intact
12 ounces milk or semi-sweet chocolate pieces
3/4 cup light cream
1-2 tablespoons Kirsch, Cointreau, brandy, or 2 teaspoons coffee

In a heavy saucepan, melt chocolate and cream over low heat, stirring until smooth. Remove from heat and blend in liqueur. Holding each berry by the stem, swirl in chocolate to partially cover and lay on waxed paper to dry. Once chocolate is hardened, arrange fruit on a silver platter. For a lively buffet table, give guests the option of dipping their own strawberries. Pour chocolate sauce into a fondue pot or chafing dish to keep warm, and place berries in a bowl for the guests to help themselves to this delightful treat.

Cafe Especial

Select a freshly ground coffee that you particularly like. Consider inventing your own blend by combining two special flavors — mix Viennese Roast with Vanilla Bean, for instance. Try out a few possible combinations before deciding on the final one to serve.

Keep the coffee piping hot in a large urn or pot set over a flame. Avoid letting the coffee boil or sit too long so that it doesn't become bitter. Stock your coffee table with a pitcher of cream, a container of hot milk, a bowl of whipped cream, a bowl of sugar cubes and tongs, and for that special touch, a dish of chocolate chips and a saucer of cinnamon sticks.

It's also a good idea to have a pot of decaffinated coffee made. Be sure not to forget the artificial sweetener and non-dairy creamer for those with special tastes. Give them a place on your table by displaying them nicely in cute containers.

COCKTAILS
AND
HORS
D'OEUVRES

Chapter 9

COCKTAILS AND
HORS D'OEUVRES

Menu

Stuffed Snow Peas   Mushrooms Florentine

Savory Artichoke Dip   Cheese Ball

Crab-filled Cherry Tomatoes   Shrimp in Prosciutto

Chicken Satés   Sweet-and-Sour Meatballs

Cheese and Paté Platter

Open Bar

Stuffed Snow Peas

48 snow peas
8 ounces cream cheese, at room temperature
1/4 cup fresh parsley, chopped
1/4 cup fresh dill, chopped
1 garlic clove, minced
black pepper (optional)

In salted, boiling water, blanch snow peas for 30 seconds. Cool in cold water, drain, and set aside. Blend the rest of the ingredients until smooth. With a sharp paring knife, split the snow peas open along the curved side. Fill each with filling, using a small spatula or pastry bag with tip.

Mushrooms Florentine
(SEE PAGE 60)

Savory Artichoke Dip

>   *2 (8 ounce) cans artichoke hearts, drained*
>   *1 cup mayonnaise*
>   *1 cup Parmesan cheese*
>   *1 small can Ortega green chilies*

Preheat oven to 350°. Blend together artichoke hearts, mayonnaise, Parmesan cheese, and green chilies, in an electric blender until smooth and creamy. Pour into shallow baking dish and bake for 20 minutes. Serve warm with small crackers.

Cheese Ball

>   *8 ounces cream cheese*
>   *3/4 cup blue cheese, crumbled*
>   *1 cup sharp Cheddar cheese, shredded*
>   *1/4 cup onion, minced*
>   *1 tablespoon Worcestershire sauce*
>   *Finely chopped parsley or nuts*

Place cheeses in a small mixing bowl and let stand at room temperature until soft. Add onion and Worcestershire sauce, mixing until fluffy. Cover and chill overnight.

Shape into a large ball and roll in parsley or nuts to cover. Chill an additional 2 hours or until firm. Set on a wooden board or platter surrounded by crackers.

Crab-filled Cherry Tomatoes

Hollow out 36 cherry tomatoes and drain upside down on paper towels. Slice a thin piece off the bottom of each tomato so that it will sit in place on serving tray.

Crab Cream Filling:

>   *1 cup crab meat, shredded*
>   *1/4 cup fresh lime juice*
>   *3 ounces cream cheese, softened*
>   *1/4 cup cream*
>   *2 tablespoons mayonnaise*
>   *1 tablespoon onions, minced*
>   *1/2 teaspoon garlic, minced*

1 teaspoon dried dill
1 teaspoon Worcestershire sauce
2 drops Tabasco sauce
salt to taste

Marinate crab meat in lime juice for 1 hour and drain well. Combine cream cheese, cream, and mayonnaise until smooth. Add to drained crab meat, blend in remaining ingredients, and mix well. Fill individual tomatoes and chill until serving time.

Shrimp in Prosciutto

40 shrimp
1/2 pound Prosciutto, thinly sliced
2 tablespoons sweet rice wine vinegar
2 tablespoons champagne vinegar
1/2 cup olive oil
2 garlic cloves, crushed

Cook shrimp in boiling water 2-3 minutes until done. Drain, cool in cold water, drain again, and set aside in glass bowl. Mix vinegars, oil and garlic. Pour over shrimp, stirring to coat thoroughly. Refrigerate overnight.

To serve, wrap each shrimp in a narrow piece of Prosciutto, overlapping edges to hold in place.

Chicken Satés

3 pounds boneless chicken breast, cut in 3/4" cubes
1 medium onion, minced
1 large fresh hot chili, seeded and chopped
3 teaspoons ginger root, minced
3 tablespoons lime juice
1 tablespoon salt
2 tablespoons soy sauce
2 tablespoons vegetable oil

In a large glass bowl, combine everything except poultry and blend well. Add chicken pieces and allow to marinate overnight in refrigerator.

Remove chicken from marinade and place on bamboo skewers, allotting two pieces per skewer. Place in shallow baking dish and pour remaining marinade over chicken. Place under broiler until cooked through. Serve warm with sauce for dipping.

Dipping Sauce:

1 cup sherry
1/4 cup brown sugar
4 tablespoons soy sauce
3 tablespoons rice wine vinegar
3 scallions, chopped

Combine sherry, sugar, soy sauce, and vinegar in a small saucepan. Cook over medium heat for 20 minutes, remove and add the scallions. Serve at room temperature.

Sweet-and-Sour Meatballs

1 1/2 pound lean ground beef
1 egg
2 tablespoons flour
1/2 teaspoon salt
1/4 teaspoon ground black pepper
1/2 cup peanut oil
1 cup chicken broth
2 large green peppers, diced
1 (8 ounce) can pineapple chunks
3 tablespoons cornstarch
1 teaspoon soy sauce
1/2 cup pineapple juice
1/2 cup vinegar
1/2 cup sugar

Shape meat into small balls. Mix egg, flour, salt, and pepper into a smooth batter. Heat peanut oil in large skillet. Dip meat balls in batter and fry until brown. Remove and keep warm. Pour off all but one tablespoon of oil and add 1/2 cup chicken broth, green pepper, and pineapple. Blend remaining ingredients and add to skillet. Cook, stirring constantly, until mixture comes to a boil and thickens. Return meat-balls to sauce and heat through. Spear each meatball with a toothpick for easy serving and arrange in chafing dish.

Cheese and Paté Platter

Purchase two types of cheese and one nice paté. Serve with a selection of whole-grain crackers or thin slices of French bread.

A
DINNER
PARTY

Chapter 10

A DINNER PARTY

Chicken and Salad Buffet

Menu

Savory Artichoke Dip   *Cheese and Paté Platter*

Asparagus and Chicken Casserole   *Honey Dijon Chicken*

Mixed Green Salad   *Carrot Soufflé*
Marinated Pasta Salad

French Bread

Mocha Charlotte

White Wine   *Coffee*

Savory Artichoke Dip
(SEE PAGE 84)

Asparagus and Chicken Casserole

> *4-5 pounds chicken breasts*
> *2 pounds fresh asparagus*
> *1/4 pound plus 2 tablespoons unsalted butter*
> *1/2 cup all-purpose flour*
> *3 cups canned low sodium broth*

1 cup half-and-half cream
3/4 pound fresh mushrooms, chopped
1/2 cup dry white wine
1 cup slivered roasted almonds
1 1/2 cups freshly grated Parmesan cheese
white pepper
salt

Place chicken breasts in water to cover and bring to a boil over high heat. Skim fat from surface, lower heat, and simmer 2-3 hours until chicken is done but still moist. Let cool in stock. Remove skin and debone, then cut into bite-size pieces. Set aside.

Cut asparagus into 1 inch pieces, discarding tough ends. Steam until not quite cooked. Drain and quickly rinse in cold water, drain again and set aside.

Melt 1/4 pound butter in a saucepan over medium heat. Stir in flour and cook about 5 minutes until bubbly, stirring continuously. Whisk in broth, then stir in cream and simmer until thickened. Add chicken, wine, mushrooms, and salt and pepper to taste.

Preheat oven to 350°. In a small saucepan, melt 2 tablespoons butter, add almonds, and cook until golden.

In a shallow 9 x 13" baking dish, combine the asparagus and chicken mixture and sprinkle with Parmesan cheese and almonds. Bake for 30 minutes, until bubbly and cheese is melted.

SERVES 8-10

Honey Dijon Chicken
(SEE PAGE 63)

Carrot Soufflé

2 cups cooked and pureed carrots
2 teaspoons lemon juice
2 tablespoons minced or grated onion
1/2 cup butter, softened
1/4 cup sugar
1 tablespoon flour
1 teaspoon salt
1/4 teaspoon cinnamon
1 cup milk
3 eggs

Preheat oven to 350°. Cook and purée carrots, add lemon juice and cover tightly until ready to assemble soufflé.

Beat all ingredients together until smooth. Pour into a 2 quart, lightly buttered soufflé or casserole dish. Bake, uncovered, for 45 minutes to 1 hour until center is firm to touch.

Marinated Pasta Salad
(SEE PAGE 62)

Mocha Charlotte

> *1 pound semi-sweet baking chocolate*
> *6 egg yolks*
> *6 egg whites*
> *1/2 cup sugar*
> *3 tablespoons instant coffee*
> *1/2 cup boiling water*
> *1 1/2 cups heavy cream, whipped*
> *1 teaspoon vanilla*
> *1/2 cup heavy cream*
> *chocolate shavings*

Melt chocolate over simmering water. Let 1/2 cup water come to a boil, add coffee, stir to dissolve and allow to cool slightly.

In a medium-sized bowl, beat egg yolks at high speed until foamy. Gradually add sugar, beating continuously until mixture is quite thick and pale yellow. Reduce speed and mix in coffee, vanilla, and melted chocolate.

With clean beaters, beat egg whites in a large bowl until they hold stiff peaks. Blend 1 cup of the beaten whites into chocolate mixture, then stir all of the chocolate into the remaining whites. Gently fold in whipped cream, stirring to thoroughly blend. Line a 9" springform pan with 24 Lady Fingers, split and brushed with 1/4 cup light rum. Overlap bottom pieces to fit pan snugly. Pour in batter and freeze up to one month.

To serve, remove from freezer 20-25 minutes before needed and remove springform sides. Whip 1/2 cup heavy cream and pile on top of the charlotte. Add chocolate shavings to garnish.

Tostada Bar

Menu

Tortilla Chips

Chili and Cheese Dip   *Guacamole*   *Bean Dip*

Chicken Ole   *Tostada Bar*

Flan

Margaritas   *Beer*

Mexican Coffee

Chili and Cheese Dip

> *2 tablespoons vegetable oil*
> *1 cup onions, chopped*
> *2 small garlic cloves, minced*
> *1 (4 ounce) can chopped green chilies*
> *2 jalapeno chilies, roasted, peeled, and chopped*
> *1 (8 ounce) can stewed tomatoes*
> *2 cups Monterey Jack cheese, shredded*
> *2 cups Cheddar cheese, shredded*
> *1 cup sour cream*

In a large saucepan, heat oil and add garlic and onions. Cook until tender but not brown. Add chilies and tomatoes, breaking up the larger pieces. Lower heat and stir in cheeses, cooking until melted. Blend in sour cream, cook until heated through but do not allow to come to a boil.

MAKES 4 CUPS

Guacamole

> *4 medium avocados*
> *2 small tomatoes, chopped*
> *4 tablespoons onion, minced*
> *2 teaspoons lemon juice*
> *1 teaspoon garlic powder*
> *1 teaspoon salt*

Peel avocados, cut in half lengthwise, and discard the seed. In a large bowl, mash the avocados with a fork until smooth. Stir in tomatoes, onion, lemon juice, garlic powder, and salt. Serve immediately.

SERVES 12-14

Bean Dip

1 (16 ounce) can refried beans
1 (4 ounce) can Ortega green chilies, diced
1 (7 ounce) can Ortega chili salsa
1 package taco seasoning
8 ounces whipped cream cheese
1 pound Cheddar cheese, grated

In a large bowl, mix together beans, chilies, salsa, taco seasoning, and cream cheese. Stir in 3/4's of the grated cheese and pour mixture into a 9 x 13 x 2" baking dish. Sprinkle with remaining cheese and bake at 350° for 30 minutes. For serving, keep dip warm in chafing dish or on a hot plate.

Chicken Olé

5 chicken breasts
1 dozen corn tortillas, cut into 1" strips
1 medium onion, diced
3 cups Cheddar cheese, grated
1 can cream of chicken soup
1 can cream of mushroom soup
1 cup milk
1 (7 ounce) can Ortega red chili salsa

Boil chicken breasts until cooked, remove skin and bones. Tear into bite-sized pieces and set aside.

Combine soups, milk, and salsa, mixing until smooth. In a large casserole dish, spread a thin coating of sauce followed by a layer of tortilla strips, a layer of chicken pieces, a covering of cheese, and a layer of onions. Continue layering in this manner, finishing with a layer of sauce. Sprinkle the top with cheese. Cover and bake at 325° for 1 hour. Remove cover and bake an additional 30 minutes.

SERVES 10-12

Tostada Bar

> 2 dozen corn tortillas
> 1 (16 ounce) can refried beans, heated
> 3 pounds lean ground beef, crumbled and fried
> 3 cups cooked and shredded chicken breast
> 1 large head of lettuce, finely shredded
> 3 cups Cheddar cheese, grated
> 3 cups tomatoes, chopped
> 2 cups sour cream
> 1 cup green onions, including tops, diced
> 3 cups guacamole
> 1 (7 ounce) can Ortega red salsa
> Oil for frying

Pour oil 1/4" deep into a medium skillet. Fry each tortilla in the hot oil until brown and crisp. Remove and drain on paper towels. Set aside until needed for party.

To serve, arrange all tostada components in a row to allow each guest to assemble her own tostada. Stack tortillas at beginning of assembly line. Place separate bowls of the following ingredients in the order that they are needed: refried beans, ground beef, chicken, lettuce, cheese, tomatoes, sour cream, green onions, guacamole, and salsa. If you are planning on having quite a few guests, arrange the ingredients in two separate rows on both ends of the buffet table.

Flan

> 3/4 cup sugar
> 1 (14 ounce) can sweetened condensed milk
> 1 cup whipping cream
> 1/2 cup milk
> 4 eggs
> 1 cinnamon stick

Melt sugar in a 7" saucepan over medium heat. Reduce heat and continue to cook, stirring occasionally. When sugar is melted and brown, immediately spoon over bottom and sides of a shallow 1 1/2 quart baking dish. Set aside while caramel cools in dish. Preheat oven to 325°.

Combine condensed milk, cream, milk, and eggs, in blender and mix thoroughly. Pour into baking dish with caramelized sugar and drop a whole cinnamon stick into the middle of the mixture.

Bake in hot water bath by positioning baking dish inside larger pan filled with hot water. Water should reach halfway up sides of baking dish. Bake 1 hour and 50 minutes or until a knife comes out clean when inserted. Check during baking in case flan is browning too quickly. If so, cover loosely with foil.

When done, cool and refrigerate at least 3 hours. To serve, run a knife around edges and invert carefully onto serving plate.

SERVES 8-10

Margaritas

1 1/4 cups freshly squeezed lime juice
1 cup tequila
1/3 cup Cointreau
1/3 cup sugar (or more, if needed)
lime wedges
coarse salt
ice cubes

Rub the rims of stemmed goblets with lime wedges. Dip the rims into a saucer filled with salt to coat edges of glasses.

Fill a blender 3/4's full with ice cubes. Pour in lime juice, tequila, and Cointreau, add sugar, and blend. Mix at high speed until mixture is frothy. Taste and add more sugar, if needed. Pour into prepared glasses and serve immediately.

MAKES 4-5 DRINKS

Mexican Coffee

1 ounce Kahlua
1/2 ounce brandy
1 teaspoon chocolate syrup
hot coffee
dash cinnamon
sweetened whipped cream

Place Kahlua, brandy, chocolate syrup, and cinnamon in coffee cup or mug. Fill with hot coffee and stir to blend. Top with whipped cream and serve immediately.

MAKES 1 DRINK

Pasta Party

Menu

Antipasto

Angel Hair Pasta with Pesto

Tagliatelli Primavera   *Italian Sausage Lasagna*

Garlic Bread

Blueberry and Peach Tartlets

Chianti

Antipasto

Antipasto is a lavish arrangement of meats, cheeses, vegetables, and condiments. In recreating this Italian delicacy, have condiments cut in bite-sized pieces and meats and cheeses thinly sliced. After slicing, roll meat slices and place seamed side down on platters. Cheese should be sliced in diagonal strips before rolling. Arrange on platter with meat and fill in with marinated mushrooms, peppers, olives, artichoke hearts, and whatever else suits your fancy.

Go to your local Italian or gourmet market to find the following antipasto ingredients:

Mozzarella
Mortadella
Provolone
Pepperoni
Salami
Prosciutto
Capicola
Hot peppers
Roasted red peppers
Marinated mushrooms
Marinated hearts of palm
Marinated artichoke hearts
Marinated olives

Angel Hair Pasta with Pesto

4 pounds angel hair pasta, cooked al dente and drained
1/2 pound whole pine nuts
1/2 cup pignolia nuts
4 garlic cloves, peeled
1 teaspoon salt
1/2 teaspoon ground pepper
3-4 cups fresh basil leaves
1/4 pound freshly grated Parmesan cheese
1/4 pound grated Romano cheese
1 1/2 - 2 cups olive oil

To make pesto, chop the nuts and garlic, add basil and continue chopping until very fine. Put into a medium bowl and add grated cheeses, salt, and pepper. Slowly pour in olive oil, mixing until creamy.

Place pasta in a large bowl. Toss with 2 cups of the pesto, reserving remainder for another use. Add whole pine nuts and toss well. Blend in additional oil and grated cheese to taste.

SERVES 18-20

Tagliatelli Primavera

4 pounds tagliatelli
3 carrots, peeled and diced
10 fresh asparagus stalks, cut into 1" pieces
10 small zucchini, diced
1 head cauliflower, broken into florets
1 head broccoli, broken into florets
1 green pepper, diced
1 red pepper, diced
3 Jerusalem artichokes, peeled and sliced
1/2 cup olive oil
1/2 cup basil, chopped
1/2 cup parsley
Parmesan cheese, grated

Cook pasta until done. Drain, rinse with cold water, and drain again. Cook all the vegetables, except peppers and artichokes, until tender but still crisp. Rinse with cold water and drain.

Toss the pasta with the vegetables. Add oil, basil, parsley, artichokes, and peppers, and sprinkle with grated cheese. Toss again.

SERVES 20-24

Italian Sausage Lasagna

> 2 tablespoons olive oil
> 1 garlic clove, chopped
> 1 onion, chopped
> 1 1/2 pounds sweet Italian sausage
> 3 cups marinara sauce
> 1 pound lasagna noodles
> 1 pound ricotta or cottage cheese
> 1 pound mozzarella cheese, thinly sliced
> 1/2 cup grated Parmesan cheese

Preheat oven to 350°. In a saucepan, sauté garlic in oil for 5 minutes. Remove sausage from casing and add to saucepan. Cook over medium heat until sausage is brown and crumbly; drain excess fat, stir in marinara sauce.

Cook lasagna noodles until done. Drain, and rinse with cold water while gently separating noodles to prevent them from sticking to each other. Cover a 9 x 13" baking dish with a thin layer of sauce, add a layer of noodles, then sauce, ricotta cheese, and mozzarella cheese. Continue layering until pan is filled, ending with sauce. Sprinkle all with Parmesan cheese. Bake 30-35 minutes until bubbly.

SERVES 12

Blueberry and Peach Tartlets

Pastry Shells:
> 1/2 pound unsalted butter, softened
> 1/2 cup sugar
> 1 egg yolk
> 1 1/2 cups flour
> pinch of salt

Filling:
> 2 cups milk
> 1 egg
> 3 egg yolks
> 1/2 cup sugar
> 6 tablespoons flour
> 1/2 teaspoon vanilla
> 1/2 cup peaches, thinly sliced
> 1/2 cup blueberries
> 2 tablespoons apricot preserves, strained

To make pastry shells, cream together butter, sugar, and salt. Add egg yolk, then flour, and mix until smooth. Form into ball, cover, and refrigerate 1 hour.

Roll dough out to 1/4" thickness and cut into 4" rounds. Press into 3" greased tart pans and refrigerate for 30 minutes.

Preheat oven to 350°. Bake empty tart shells for 10 minutes, until golden brown. Set aside to cool.

To make filling, bring milk to a boil in a saucepan, and allow to cool. Cream the egg, egg yolks, and sugar together. Add in flour, vanilla, and a little of the hot milk to blend. Add the egg mixture to the pan and cook, stirring continuously, until thick and smooth like custard. Remove from heat, cover with wax paper, and let cool.

Fill tart shells half-full with cooled custard. Top filling with peaches and blueberries to cover.

Mix apricot preserves with water, bring to boil, and strain to make 2 tablespoons. Cool and brush over fruit to glaze.

MAKES 12

ORGANIZING
THE
SHOWER

Chapter 11

ORGANIZING THE SHOWER

Now that you've had a chance to explore the wide variety of themes, styles, and types of showers available, it's finally time to get down to basics with your own event and commit your decisions to writing. The following work sheets, which will help you organize all your party details from your menu to the well-stocked bar, are designed to make the process as painless as possible.

- **Menu and beverage work sheet** — food and drinks are central to your party's success. Planning helps keep you within your budget.

- **Bar checklist** — these items plus a smile will be everything you'll need for a great bar.

- **Party equipment checklist** — all the necessities imaginable to make sure you're ready.

- **Decorating and supplies work sheet** — these are the small and not-so-small touches that will give your shower its flair.

Menu and Beverage Work Sheet

Number of Guests _____

Type of Shower: ☐ Sit Down ☐ Buffet ☐ Brunch
       ☐ Luncheon ☐ A Victorian Tea ☐ Dessert Party
       ☐ Cocktails & Hors d'Oeuvres ☐ Dinner Party

Hors d'Oeuvres:_____
_____
_____
_____

Salads:_____
_____
_____
_____

Main Course:_____
_____
_____
_____

Other Dishes:_____
_____
_____
_____

Desserts:_____
_____
_____
_____

Beverages:_____
_____
_____
_____

104

Bar Checklist

Bar Equipment
Ice bucket
Ice tongs
Ice pick
Sharp knife
Corkscrew
Bottle opener
Jigger measures
Large mixing pitcher
Long handled spoon
Mixing glass
Shaker/strainer
Blender
Lemon/lime squeezer
Coasters or cocktail napkins

Bar Accompaniments
Ice (1/2 to 3/4 lbs. per person)
Lemons, limes, oranges
Green olives
Cocktail onions
Lemon zester
Cocktail toothpicks

Mixers
Perrier
Club soda
Tonic
Ginger ale
Soft drinks
Orange and tomato juices
Bloody Mary mix

Liquor
Rum: 1 light & 1 dark
Bourbon
Gin
Vodka
Scotch
Blended Whiskey
Dry Vermouth
Sweet Vermouth

Liqueurs
Amaretto
Bailey's Irish Cream
Cognac
Cassis
Cointreau
Dubonnet
Frangelico
Grand Marnier
Kahlua

Beer
Light beer
Dark beer

Wines
White wine
Red wine
Champagne
Port
Dry Sherry
Cream Sherry

Party Equipment Checklist

Use the following checklist to keep track of all the party equipment you'll need.

Items	Size	Number Needed	Have (✓)
Banquet Tables: 4', 6', 8' long			
Round Tables:			
36" dia. seats 4-6			
48" dia. seats 6			
54" dia. seats 8			
60" dia. seats 10			
Misc. Tables			
Folding Chairs			
Umbrellas			
Portable Barbecue			
Lattices			
Heaters			
Tiki Torches			
Lighting			
Banquet Tablecloths			
Circular Tablecloths			
Napkins			
China:			
Dinner Plate			
Luncheon Plate			
Salad Plate			
Cup and Saucer			
Creamer and Sugar			
Serving Platters			
Serving Bowls 9"			
Wine Glasses			
Champagne Glasses			
Water Goblets			
Cordials, Shot Glasses			

Party Equipment Checklist (continued)

Items	Size	Number Needed	Have (✓)
Hi Ball Glasses: 8 oz., 12 oz.			
Water Pitcher			
Salt & Pepper Shaker Set			
Punch Bowl with Ladle			
Glass Serving Bowl, 9"			
4 Tier Serving Tray			
Chafing Dish with Sterno			
Coffee Maker			
Coffee Urn, Stainless or Silver			
Silver Coffee Server			
Silverware:			
Dinner Fork			
Salad Fork			
Dessert Fork			
Dinner Knife			
Spoons			
Serving Fork			
Serving Spoon			
Pastry Trays			
Salad Tongs			
Ice Tongs			
Cake Knife			
Cake or Pie Server			
Silver Tongs			
Bread Baskets			
Table Top Stoves: 2, 3 or 4 Burner			
4' Bars and Back Bar Table			
Bar Buckets			
Bar Towles			
Ice Tub			

Decorating and Supplies Work Sheet

Invitations:	Type, Color, Size, Amount, etc.	✓
Preprinted		
Fabric paint		
Supplies:		
Decorations:		
Balloons		
Baskets		
Streamers, Banners		
Flowers		
Candles		
Other:		
Table Supplies:		
Paper Tablecloth		
Napkins		
Cups		
Plastic Utensils		
Place Cards		
Party Favors		
Other:		
Games:		
Pencils, sharpened		
Paper or Note Pads		
Stopwatch or Egg Timer		
Items to Play the Game		
Party Prizes		
Other:		

BRIDAL SHOWER THEMES

Chapter 12

BRIDAL SHOWER THEMES

Bridal showers are even more fun when they have a theme which determines the type of gifts to bring. If the bride-to-be already has a household of her own, it would be wise to consult with her regarding her preference. Once you have settled on a theme, you can start planning your decorations accordingly. Be sure to include your choice on the invitation itself.

The following themes can be combined with invitation, decorating, and party favor ideas from previous chapters. Mix and match your favorites to create a distinctive shower.

A Miscellaneous Shower

True to its name, anything and everything goes with this popular shower! Guests are free to bring whatever they wish in the way of gifts. Despite the increasing popularity of theme showers, the miscellaneous shower is still the most common. It works especially well for the co-ed party. Although there is no designated gift theme, a decorating theme can still be set. Choose whatever appeals to you, from a Victorian tea to a tostada party — any and all food and decorating choices are acceptable. Increase eye appeal by choosing terrific linens, dramatic centerpieces, and interesting party favors. Spending less time on a theme lets you go all out on your decorations!

A Gift Basket Shower

This is one of my favorites! Each guest brings a basket, box, or container filled with imaginative goodies for a designated area of the house. It allows your guests to be creative in their selection of items to get the bride off to a good start. Opening the baskets involves everyone in the fun as they watch the wide variety of goodies selected. You can either tell each guest the theme of her particular basket or leave it to the discretion of the individual. In that case, it might be helpful to include a list of basket content suggestions to choose from. When they RSVP, they can also tell you which basket they've chosen to bring.

Make this shower an afternoon luncheon by packing individual box lunches consisting of quiche, sandwiches, pasta salads, chips, and giant brownies for dessert. You can also use wicker lap trays and have the guests serve themselves from a buffet table.

Basket Fillers

Kitchen Basket — Pile a colander or fruit basket with a variety of small kitchen goodies. Look for a grater, mushroom brush, potato peeler, pot holders, and kitchen magnets, all in bright and cheery colors.

Bathroom Basket — Use a cute wastepaper basket to carry nice soaps, bath salts, loofah sponges, fragrant lotions, and luscious bath oils. Cushion your surprises with unusual washcloths or guest towels.

Wedding Accessories Basket — Help the bride gather the necessary items she will need on her special day. Using a pastel wicker desk tray, choose one or more of the following items to get her started on her accessories: a cake knife and server set, toasting glasses, a special pen and lace-trimmed guest book, a frilly garter, and a dainty handkerchief. To make your search a breeze, send for the free catalogue of the Beverly Clark Collection of Exquisite Bridal Accessories. Write to:

> The Beverly Clark Collection
> 12021 Wilshire Blvd. Suite 208
> Los Angeles, CA 90025
>
> Or phone: (213) 396-1992

Laundry Basket — Find the cutest hamper or laundry basket you can and stock it with clothes pins, soap, bleach, spot remover, starch, and a travel iron.

Gourmet Food Basket — Spoil the bride-to-be with an assortment of delicious food. You can center your basket around a particular food. Select a coffee and teas basket, a pasta basket, a sweets basket with cookies and marmalades, or a wine and cheese basket. The possibilities are endless.

Spice Basket — Be responsible for the spice in her life by starting your girlfriend off with a tempting selection of spices. Choose pretty bottles to scatter throughout the basket or place in a spice rack.

Baking Basket — Take a large mixing bowl to hold teaspoons, a measuring cup, spatula, egg beater, flour sifter, and a miniature muffin tin.

Sewing Basket — Even the bride who is all-thumbs will appreciate having the basics in her new household. Supply a sewing basket with a measuring tape, scissors, thread, straight pins, and a jar of buttons. For the bride who loves to sew, add personalized labels for her to sew into her creations (can be ordered from sewing stores.)

Picnic Basket — A few guests may want to pitch in for this one. Either assemble your own or indulge in one already made up.

Hobby Basket — Add this basket to your list if the bride has a favorite hobby such as painting, playing tennis, or gardening.

These are just a few of the many creative and useful baskets you can dream up — have fun thinking of more!

A Kitchen Shower

Every home depends on a well-equipped kitchen to run smoothly. There are a number of can't-do-without items that are fun to both give and receive. Since many couples already have a good start on kitchen essentials, talk to the bride to see what they both already have. Make a list of the essentials they are lacking, as well as gadgets that they particularly want. Enclose your list with each invitation to take some of the guesswork out of gift-giving.

Decorations

Keep your party centered around the kitchen — send out potholder or kitchen towel invitations (SEE INVITATIONS) and present guests with kitchen magnets for party favors. Think of wearing your favorite apron during the party and giving one to the bride the minute she walks through the door. Set your table in style, using kitchen towels as place mats with coordinating dishcloths as napkins. Create an unusual centerpiece out of small kitchen tools jauntily stuck in a ceramic container. Wooden spoons, a potato masher, an egg beater, a rolling pin, and spatulas are colorful items to be used as part of a centerpiece and then given to the bride.

The perfect motif for an all-ladies luncheon or dinner, you can decide to lay the buffet out on a kitchen counter or stove. The logical choice for elegant serving containers has to be your best and brightest mixing bowls, pots and pans, canisters, and cookie jars!

measuring spoons and cups
spatulas
rotary egg beater
potato peeler
small vegetable brush
rolling pin
square cake tins
muffin tins
grater
tea strainer
saucepans
skillets
egg poacher
meat thermometer
ladle
nut grinder
egg slicer
butter cube cutter
ice cream scoop
lettuce spinner
kitchen timer
teakettle
quiche dish
popcorn popper
deep fryer
espresso coffee maker
waffle iron
crockpot
toaster oven
juicer
salad bowl
spice rack cookbook holder

flour sifter
wooden spoons
manual can opener
potato masher
set of mixing bowls
round pie plates
cookie sheet
loaf pans
colander
set of cutting knives
double boiler
omelette pan
roasting pan
butter or sauce brush
garlic press
copper molds
cheese slicer
cake decorating kit
vegetable steamer
wire whisks
melon baller
souffle dish
electric blender
electric hand mixer
electric coffee maker
toaster
electric carving knife
electric skillet
automatic can opener
wok
carving board

A Recipe Shower

A recipe shower is the place for all the cooks to shine as each guest brings her favorite recipe affixed to an item or two required in its preparation.

Send each invitation with its own set of instructions and a recipe card to be filled out. Ask each guest to neatly write out the list of ingredients and cooking directions for one of her favorite culinary delights. The gift she chooses should have something to do with the preparation of her favorite recipe. The attached recipe cards will later be placed in a special recipe box purchased by the hostess. Many recipe boxes come already supplied with cute matching index cards for recipes. Include these or make your own after measuring the recipe box you want to use.

A recipe shower is a nice choice for a brunch or dinner. Use general decorations or rely on the ideas presented in the section on kitchen showers. You can make up menus to use as cute place mats and give recipe holders as party favors!

Be sure that your gifts match your recipes. Here are a few combinations to get you started:

Blueberry Muffins — two muffin tins wrapped in over-sized bright napkins

Quiche — a cheese grater and ceramic quiche dish

Chocolate Chip Cookies — two cookie sheets holding a bag of chocolate chips, a spatula, and colorful paper napkins

Belgian Waffles — a Belgian waffle iron and a bottle of pure maple syrup

Custard Surprise — six custard cups with tiny custard spoons

Delicious Apple Pie — a ceramic pie plate and a rolling pin

Double Trouble Chocolate Cake — mixing bowls with a battery-powered flour sifter

Terrific Lasagna — a baking dish and a manual pasta maker

A Lingerie Shower

With its lace and frills, this is the perfect shower to have at a Victorian tea. Use fresh flowers for your centerpiece and accent everything with your finest linens, silver, and serving pieces. Potpourri sachets for party favors provide a nice touch at each place setting.

For those more adventurous hostesses, try kidnapping the bride for an early morning breakfast surprise or get nostalgic and make it a pajama party!

A lingerie shower is great for the second-time bride or the woman who already has a completely stocked kitchen.

Lingerie Gift Ideas

night gowns	robes
teddies	bras
slips	lacy underwear
camisoles	stockings
lingerie bags	stocking holder
drawer and closet sachets	fabric-covered hangers
slippers	jewelry bags for travel
laundry bag	night shirt

A Linen Shower

With great decorator designs to choose from, linens are no longer a boring necessity but have become an exciting part of the bridal trousseau.

Linens can be quite expensive so do keep finances in mind when planning this shower. Many linen showers are just for the bride's relatives who would plan on giving more costly shower gifts anyway. It is also possible to have the bride register for her preferred colors and patterns so that guests may purchase individual parts of a set — one friend can buy the flat sheet, another the pillow cases, and so forth. Another alternative is to have the guests pool their money so that a small group of friends could purchase a tablecloth with another being responsible for matching napkins.

Unless the bride has decided to register for her linens, be sure to specify table and bed sizes, as well as the colors of her prospective kitchen, bath, and bedroom on the invitation. Send out printed invitations or white cloth napkins as a creative alternative (SEE INVITATIONS.)

You may choose to make this an afternoon, ladies-only party or a co-ed evening event, since all the gifts will be for both the bride and groom. Select your favorite style and decorate accordingly.

Gifts for the Linen Closet

tablecloth	napkins
place mats	silver napkin holder
silver napkin rings	sheets
pillow cases	blankets
comforter	pillow covers
mattress pad	pillows
dust ruffle and pillow shams	beach towels
bath, hand, and face towels	guest towels
bath mat	kitchen towels
dishcloths	kitchen rug

An Around-the-clock Shower

The around-the-clock shower combines the best of two different showers into one — you have the variety of a miscellaneous shower and the fun of having a theme to build your party around.

The guests are each assigned a specific time of day on their invitations. They must then select a gift appropriate for their designated time. In the instructions you have included on the invitation, be sure to ask the guests to write the time of day the gift is for on a small gift tag and attach it to the present. This way the bride sees and announces the time of day before opening the gift.

Distribute the hours according to the number of guests and the times of day that you think are the most appropriate. Friends may also attach a short note to the gift explaining exactly what they think that the bride will be doing at the designated time. These notes are usually funny rather than serious and liven up the gift opening.

Make clock invitations to send out (SEE INVITATIONS) and decorate your party room with clocks and calendars. Use pages from a large desktop calendar as place mats. Pass out fun, inexpensive watches, appointment books, or cute egg timers for party favors.

Timely Gift Suggestions

Morning Hours

alarm clock	bathrobe
electric curlers	make-up bag with brushes
lit make-up mirror	breakfast cookbook
warming basket for rolls	waffle iron
omelette pan	coffee maker
mugs and mug tree	electric kettle

Midday

appointment book	calendar
address book	pen and pencil set
blouse	earrings
slip	hair clips
wallet	purse
telephone message center	answering machine

For the non-working woman, select items more appropriate for the house — mid-day often means laundry, cleaning the house, cooking, or indulging in a hobby.

Evening Hours

bottle of wine and two glasses	cocktail shaker
cooking utensils	dessert cookbook
brandy snifters	theater tickets
certificate for hot fudge sundaes	bath oil
lingerie	classical records
a video cassette	two great novels
monopoly game	a backgammon board

A Honeymoon Shower

The perfect way to say "bon voyage" to the happy couple, this prenuptial party will supply them with a variety of travel accessories for their wedding trip. A honeymoon shower may be the ideal choice for that co-ed gathering or a fantastic way to salute the second-time bride. Plan a buffet with the couple's honeymoon destination in mind, featuring a culinary delight from that region of the world. Let your decorations show how the couple will be traveling, as well as their destination. Centerpieces can cheerfully contain toy trains, miniature cars, plastic boats, and cardboard busses. Turn to travel posters, maps, and world globes to set the mood of your party. If the couple is bound for Hawaii, don't forget to scatter a lei or two around the room. You may want to finish off your decorating by playing the type of music popular where they will be going.

No matter where they're headed or how they are getting there, thoughtful gifts will always come in handy.

Just-the-ticket Gifts

travel alarm clock	guidebooks
rolls of film	travel diary
photo album	luggage cart on wheels
travel iron	plastic-lined make-up bag
travel shaving kit	jewelry roll
shoe bags	lingerie bag
laundry kit with line and clips	nail kit
first aid kit	sun lotion
beach towels	travel games
hanging garment bag	carry-on luggage
travel hair dryer	travel electric curlers

And for those bound for a foreign country:

leather passport case
money roll or belt
foreign current converter and adapter
foreign language phrase book
small amount of foreign currency traveler's checks
pocket calculator

A Hobby Shower

For the couple who already has all the essentials, this is a great choice! It also solves the problem of what to give the second-time bride or the lady who is being honored with several showers.

This one lends itself nicely to the co-ed celebration, especially if the couple shares a hobby. Play the sleuth and find out what both like to do in their spare time. Compile a list of their leisure time activities, which will be the basis of your party. Be sure to include the list with each invitation, carefully delineating who likes to do what. Maybe they both enjoy gardening, hiking, skiing, golfing, tennis, or bike riding. She may also like to sew, knit, or paint where he is the born fisherman. Knowing what they enjoy will supply you with endless decorating ideas. You can be as elaborate or as simple as you wish. Encourage your guests to bring small accessories and if the selections are funny, so much the better!

An Entertaining Shower

As its title says, this one is geared toward the bride who has already collected the basics and is now looking forward to entertaining in her new home.

Definitely designed for couples, the entertaining shower is perfect for a Sunday brunch, an exciting cocktail party, or an elegant dinner affair. They all create the ideal setting to shower the new couple with those special gifts guaranteed to make entertaining a breeze.

It's not necessary to have a particular decorating theme since the party itself is the theme — entertaining and doing it in style is the feeling of this one.

A group of friends may want to join forces and purchase a card table and folding chairs, punch bowl set, or elegant chafing dish to get the couple off to a good start.

Other Entertaining Thoughts

cheese board and slicer	relish dish
chips and dip set	fondue pot
electric warming tray	popcorn popper
nut and candy dishes	serving trays
bar glasses	ice bucket with tongs
wine glasses	bottle opener
cocktail shaker and jigger	martini pitcher
wine rack	silver-plated coasters
ashtrays	playing cards
pair of dice	board games
barbecue utensils	his and her's aprons

A Gourmet Shower

Here's another one for the bride or couple who seems to have everything! Gourmet delights are everywhere, so there is no end to the number of delicious treats you can come up with for this party! Combine this idea with the basket theme by having each guest bring his food gift in a basket, decorative tin, bowl, or imaginative container.

Consider really spoiling your guests and yourself by making it a decadent dessert party! Use your best linens, china, and silver. Continue pampering everyone by presenting them with chocolate swans or truffles packed in tiny gold boxes to take home.

More-than-gourmet Baskets

- Give gourmet popcorn tucked into a personalized popcorn bowl or affixed to an air popper.

- Prepare a sumptuous assortment of preserves, jams, and honey snuggled in a wicker basket.

- Select a waffle iron with a sweet variety of delectable syrups — pure maple, boysenberry, raspberry, etc.

- Treat the couple to their own copy of a chocolate lover's cookbook. Decorate lavishly with a supply of Belgian chocolates and homemade fudge.

- Line a breadbasket with a cheery checked hand towel, add a pasta maker and fill with an assortment of special sauces, Italian olive oil, and fine vinegars.

- Let your honored couple know the scoop by presenting them with a silver-plated ice cream scoop. Don't forget to top it all off with the gooiest treats you can find — fudge, caramel, and marshmallow toppings with a jar of maraschino cherries for good measure!

- Stuff your finest container with an appetizing assortment of imported cheeses, tinned pates, caviar, and sardines. Tuck in a variety of unusual crackers and complete with a jar of stuffed olives.

BRIDAL
SHOWER
GAMES
AND GIFTS

Chapter 13

BRIDAL SHOWER
GAMES AND GIFTS

*S*hower entertainment usually centers around socializing, games, and opening the gifts. Depending on your guests, the formality of your party, and your own preferences, you may decide to eliminate the games or relegate them to a relatively minor role in the festivities. To fill the gap, think of hiring a magician, palm reader, or psychic to entertain those special guests. For a co-ed event, you might want to think in terms of a stand-up comedian or juggler to add pizazz to your party.

Music

An essential ingredient in creating and sustaining a comfortable mood, music must suit the occasion. Think in terms of soft background music supplied by tapes or records. A low volume guarantees that your guests will have a comfortable background for conversation but yet won't have to strain to be heard. A special theme begs for special music. Choose a mariachi band to liven up a tostada party, a pair of strolling fiddlers for an Italian pasta fling.

In keeping with the more sophisticated air of the cocktail party or formal dinner, engage a flutist, pianist, or guitarist for entertainment and forego the games. If you want couples to dance, think of renting a jukebox, hiring a disc jockey, or featuring a local band. Music academies, high schools, and community colleges are all excellent sources of good musicians willing to work at reasonable rates. You can also browse through the classified ads of local newspapers and magazines. Don't forget to check the most reliable source you have — your friends.

Games

Bridal Gown Designer

This one calls for some imagination, so let's see how creative your guests can be! Divide the group into two or three teams and place each in a separate room. Supply each of the three teams with several rolls of toilet paper. The teams select their own "bride," and prepare to design an original gown for her out of the toilet paper they have. No tape or pins are allowed. Give your designers about 15-20 minutes to complete their creations and then have everyone except the team brides reassemble in the living room. Call out each team's entry to model for the real bride. She has the honor of choosing the winning team which has fashioned the most creative dress. Each member of the winning team receives a small prize for her efforts.

High Roller

This is a lively game suitable for any size group. Arrange the guests' chairs in a circle, piling an assortment of wrapped gifts in the center on the floor. Buy one gift for every four to five guests and wrap enticingly. Make each one appear completely different from all the others. Select small items, such as a powder puff or make-up brush, to go into the largest, most expensive-looking boxes while you place nicer gifts in "plain Jane" wrappings. Try to pick out prizes that vary widely in size, length, weight, or width. Use two sets of dice (or three, if there are more than 20 players) and pick two players sitting across from each other to start the game. Each gets one roll. If the person rolls doubles, a gift from the center can be selected. When all the gifts have been taken from the center, doubles allows the gambler to pluck a package off someone's lap — this is where the fun really begins! After one roll, the dice are passed to the left. Set the timer for seven minutes and when it goes off, whoever has a present gets to keep it.

Be sure that the winners unwrap their gifts while still seated in the circle — everyone will be surprised at the real contents of each gift! Most often it turns out that the gift everyone seemed to be fighting over is really the silliest present of the bunch! A good game for co-ed parties, take care to ensure that the items you select are appropriate for both sexes.

Tell Me Who I Am

A perfect starter activity, this game is a great way to get your guests to begin to mingle. Prepare ahead of time by writing the name of a famous person, celebrity, singer, or author on a 3 x 5" index card. As each guest arrives, pin one of the secret identities on her back without divulging the name on the card. The task is for the guests to find out exactly who they are by asking others questions which can only be answered with a yes or no. Everyone will begin to mingle in an effort to discover their own identity! The first one to figure out correctly who she is wins. If you've got a super sleuth at the party who guesses correctly almost right away, you may want to continue the game and award second and third prizes.

Whose Face Is That?

Tear 10-15 pictures of brides out of a magazine. Then carefully cut out each face, leaving the surrounding hair, neck, and ears. Look through other magazines and newspapers for close-ups of both male and female notorieties and cut out their faces. Give the brides new faces by taping the celebrity cut-outs carefully in place with scotch tape. Give each contestant a paper and pencil. As you hold up each new "bride" your guests need to determine just whose face that really is. The one with the most correct guesses wins.

Clothespin Game

Your guests will enjoy having this one pinned on them! As party guests arrive, clip a clothespin somewhere on their clothes and instruct them that crossing their legs is not allowed for the entire party. If one guest catches another crossing her legs, that person gets to take the guilty party's clothespin and add it to her own collection. If a person transgresses while wearing several clothespins she has captured from other guests, she loses them all. The person with the most clips at the end of the party is declared the winner.

Fill In the Blanks

Each guest receives a pencil and a piece of paper. The sheet contains the word "bridal" written vertically down the left margin with the word "shower" directly across from it on the right side. The object of the game is to use each pair of letters as the beginning and end of the longest word you can think of. The first word, for example, must begin with "b" and end with "s." Numerous possibilities include words such as "brides" or "bouquets." Each letter in the newly created word is worth one point, unless the word pertains directly to a wedding or shower, in which case each letter brings two points. Give everyone ten minutes to rack their brains for words. The one with the most points wins.

The Newlywed Game

Based on the television show, "The Newlywed Game," this party time favorite works well for either a co-ed or all-ladies party. The game will take a little more preparation on your part but the results are worth it! Call the groom ahead of time and quiz him about himself and his relationship with his intended. Be sure that whatever you ask him remains a secret so that the bride doesn't know anything ahead of time. List all of your questions on 3 x 5" cards and write the groom's answers on the back of each. Here are a few questions to start you out:

- "Where did you go on your first date?"
- "What did she wear the first time you saw her?"
- "What was your last fight about?"
- "What's your favorite dish that she cooks?"
- "Which habit of hers annoys you the most?"

Make sure that you have asked enough questions so that each person attending the party will have something to ask the bride. To start the game, distribute one card to each guest and have the bride or couple sit in front of the group. Each person then reads the question from her individual card. The bride is not allowed to answer yet but has to wait until all the questions are read. After everyone has had a chance to hear all the questions that will be asked of the bride, have them guess the number of questions that they think the bride will be able to answer correctly and write down their estimates in a corner of their index card. Now the bride can begin to answer the questions one at a time. Each guest reads her question, waits for the bride's answer, and then reads the groom's response written on the back of the card. After the bride has given all her answers, tally up her correct responses to see how well she knows her husband-to-be. A prize goes to the guest who comes closest to estimating the number of correct answers.

Take My Advice

Since we all think that we give the best advice, everyone should enjoy this game which gives your guests a chance to really shine as marriage experts. Preprint sheets with a list of 12 "hot" topics on which the guests are to give their advice. Each sentence must start with the word already there ("never" or "always") and should be the guest's own "little gem of wisdom." Feel free to add any other areas of domestic life where you feel the bride might like a few tips. The funnier the advice, the better. The first contestant to finish wins, and gets to share all her advice with the group.

1. (Fighting) Always_____.

2. (Cooking) Never _____.

3. (Laundry) Always_____.

4. (Cleaning) Never _____.

5. (Shopping) Always _____ .

6. (Kissing) Never_____ .

7. (Fighting) Always_____ .

8. (Old Boyfriends) Never _____ .

9. (Money) Always _____ .

10. (Work) Never _____ .

11. (Honesty) Always_____ .

12. (In-Laws) Never _____ .

Stock Your Kitchen

Give each person a pencil and paper and ask them to furnish the bride's kitchen with as many items as they can think of. The only catch is that each object listed must begin with a letter contained in the bride's first name. Allow two to three minutes thinking time per letter and declare the one with the longest list of kitchen goodies the winner.

It's In The Bag ╱

A true scavenger hunt that will take your party goers no further than their handbags! Tell your guests to be brave and dig deep in their purses to find as many of the listed items as possible. Items cannot be counted twice, no matter how many of them you actually have. For example, whether your hand bag contains one or five stamps, you still win five points. 10-15 minutes should be ample time for your company to have successfully struggled through the contents of their handbags and resurfaced with ample points. The scavenger with the most points (and messiest bag!) wins.

NAME_____ TOTAL POINTS_____

Postage Stamp	5 pts._____	Chewing Gum	5 pts._____
Aspirin	10 pts._____	Pen	3 pts._____
Pencil	5 pts._____	Matches	5 pts._____
Bobby Pins	2 pts._____	Address Book	15 pts._____
Lipstick	5 pts._____	Tissues	25 pts._____
Hand Lotion	10 pts._____	Nail File	15 pts._____
Nail Polish	25 pts._____	Hair Brush	3 pts._____
Hair Clip	2 pts._____	Eyelash Curler	50 pts._____
Rubber Band	10 pts._____	Mirror	5 pts._____
Tweezers	10 pts._____	Eye Glasses	10 pts._____
Coin Purse	10 pts._____	Children Photos	5 pts._____
Breath Mints	15 pts._____	Library Card	15 pts._____
Toothbrush	25 pts._____	Credit Card	5 pts._____

Wedding Scramble

Find out just how your guests would go about organizing a wedding by having them unscramble the following list of necessary wedding "ingredients." All the tangled names are things and people commonly found at both ceremony and reception. The first person finished wins. If no one finishes in 10 minutes, award the prize to the person with the most correct answers.

1. MORGO _____
2. GRIN _____
3. GREALCMNY _____
4. RESHUS _____
5. TAREGR _____
6. SMIEDSIBRAD _____
7. STIGF _____
8. WORFSEL _____
9. KACE _____
10. TENBAMS _____
11. REBID _____
12. CREI _____

The Correct Answers to Wedding Scramble

1. GROOM
2. RING
3. CLERGYMAN
4. USHERS
5. GARTER
6. BRIDESMAIDS
7. GIFTS
8. FLOWERS
9. CAKE
10. BEST MAN
11. BRIDE
12. RICE

Picture This

Similar to the lively game of "Pictionary," our wedding shower version is designed to get everyone involved. Divide the group into two teams (SEE DIRECTIONS BELOW) and have each team select an "artist," who will be responsible for drawing a picture while the rest of the team will try to guess what it means. The hostess prepares for the game by writing down sentences on slips of paper describing activities that the new bride will be doing, before, during and after the wedding. Choose any of the following activities or make up your own: selecting a bridal gown, walking down the aisle, doing the laundry, cooking dinner, watching T.V., mowing the lawn, writing thank-you notes, and clipping store coupons. Place all the slips in a large hat. At the start of each round, the two team artists draw a slip out of the hat. On the word "Go!" they open their slips, read their sentences, and rush to their team to begin drawing the activity written on their slip. The first team to guess correctly what their team sketcher has drawn, wins that round. The losers of the round become spectators. After the first round, the winners are again divided into two separate groups to begin a second round. The new groups again select artists and the game begins once more. If you have enough guests, the winners of the second round can be divided into another two teams for the third and final round of competition. The winners of this play-off round are then each given a prize. Adjust the number of rounds according to the number of guests playing. A small group will have only two rounds, a larger probably four.

How to Divide the "Picture This" teams (For 24 Guests)

1. Have both pink and white construction paper ready. Cut out 12 pink and 12 white 1 x 4" slips and separate into two piles.

2. On three of the white and three of the pink slips write: "BRIDE, RING."

3. On three of the white and three of the pink slips write: "BRIDE, BOUQUET."

4. On three of the white and three of the pink slips write: "GROOM, RING."

5. On three of the white and three of the pink slips write: "GROOM, BOUQUET."

6. Everybody draws one of these slips from a hat and two teams, one white and one pink are formed.

7. At the end of round 1, either the pink or the white team wins. At this point the winning team redivides into two new teams - BRIDES vs GROOMS.

8. The third and final round will be played between the RINGS and the BOUQUETS.

Complete The Sentence

Each guest will received a printed sheet of paper containing sentences that need to be completed. Allot only five minutes for this one — the contestant with the greatest number of correctly completed sentences wins!

1. A woman's work _____.

2. A happy house_____.

3. Behind every great man_____.

4. A woman's place _____.

5. When the going gets tough _____.

6. A stitch in time _____.

7. My house is _____.

8. The path of true love_____.

9. Variety is _____.

10. Every man's home _____.

11. True love _____.

12. Marriages are _____.

13. A watched pot _____.

14. If the shoe fits_____.

15. A penny saved _____.

16. Home is_____.

17. Too many cooks _____.

ANSWERS TO SENTENCE COMPLETION

1. is never done.
2. is full of laughter.
3. is a successful woman.
4. is in the home.
5. the tough get going (or the wife goes shopping!)
6. saves nine.
7. your house.
8. never runs smooth.
9. the spice of life.
10. is his castle.
11. conquers all.
12. made in heaven.
13. never boils.
14. wear it.
15. is a penny earned.
16. where the heart is.
17. spoil the broth.

Prize-winning Ideas

Be sure that you have stocked up on plenty of prizes. Have one for each game plus a few in reserve in case of ties. When planning a co-ed shower, make sure that the prizes are neutral!

address book	memo pads
day planner	key chains
gourmet chocolate	jewelry roll for travel
make-up brush	coffee mugs
pound of specialty coffee beans	bottle of wine
corkscrew	flavored popcorn in a tin
ice cream store gift certificate	miniature stuffed animal
potpourri and drawer sachets	scarfs
ring dishes	small woven baskets with lids
bath salts	special soaps
jams and jellies	exotic cheese and crackers
gift certificate for a car wash	pocket dictionary
cassette	telephone message pad
two movie passes	paperback books

Opening the Gifts

For gift opening with a twist, have a secretly selected secretary write down exactly what the bride says when she opens each gift. After all the presents have been opened, read the quotes out loud. It's surprising and fun!

Be sure to designate the helpers — you need someone to keep track of the gifts and who they were given by. Also someone can be appointed to make a bouquet out of the ribbons and bows from all the packages. For a simple yet fun bouquet, use a paper plate with an X cut in the center. Draw the ribbons through the slit, gathering the bows into a colorful bunch on the plate. Add your stick-on bows around the center grouping to cover the entire plate, making the bride's first bouquet! Later this fun bouquet can be the stand-in flowers at the wedding rehearsal.

PLANNING
A
BABY
SHOWER

Chapter 14

PLANNING A BABY SHOWER

Whether she is expecting her first or second baby, every mother is thrilled to have her friends help her get ready to welcome her new bundle of joy into the world. Even though there is speculation as to the exact origins of this gentle custom, it is generally believed that it was an outgrowth of the desire of friends to honor an expectant mother while helping the young couple cope with the added expense of a newborn.

Who Hosts a Shower

In contrast to the etiquette surrounding a bridal shower, it is appropriate for any well-wisher, even the grandmother-to-be, to honor the expectant mother. Most baby showers are hosted by a sister, best friend, or close group of friends.

Who Is Invited

Traditionally showers have been women-only celebrations. Today, however, baby showers enjoy an expanded format which can include the proud fathers-to-be in the celebration. When planning your special event, check with the mother whether or not she thinks that her husband and other important male friends and relatives would enjoy being part of the festivities. Whether it's an up-to-date co-ed affair or a strictly ladies party with lots of time for oohing and ahhing over adorable baby gifts, hosting a baby shower is lots of fun!

In the case of a surprise shower, plan on consulting with the guest of honor's mother and husband. You will need a list of her special friends and relatives to be included, as well as a rundown on those gift items she needs or would especially like to have.

Choosing the Date and Location

Plan your shower for four to six weeks before the mother's due date. In the case of "Coming Out" or "First Month Birthday" parties, you'll want to wait until after the little one has made his appearance. Be careful not to plan your party too close to the due date as babies are unpredictable and tend to put in early appearances when everyone least expects it! Also, the closer the mother is to her due date, the more tired she usually is. If many friends and relatives will be coming in from out of town, plan your party for a month or two after the birth, to allow those special guests to visit with both mom and the newborn at the same time.

Baby showers are usually held in the home of the hostess and are generally scheduled for a weekend day or evening.

Selecting the Type and Time

When settling on the type of shower you want to give, keep both your budget, your house, and your guests in mind. If the majority of guests are wives and mothers themselves, it's a good idea to schedule an all-ladies event during the day, reserving a weekend evening party for the celebration designed for couples.

A late morning brunch, luncheon, afternoon tea, and dessert party are all great when considering gathering all your girlfriends together. If you are considering a co-ed event, it's better to lean toward a cocktail and hors d'oeuvres party or a casual buffet dinner. Let the time of the party be determined by the type of party you're striving to give.

Invitations

Although guests can be invited by telephone, it's preferable to send out written invitations three to four weeks in advance. Let your carefully chosen invitation set the mood for the type of party you have planned. Look through the dazzling array of preprinted invitations readily available or opt for some fun by designing your own. Either way, be sure that you include a small map or written directions to the party, as well as the telephone number of the house.

An Offer They Can't Refuse — Invitations With a Flair

- Send a diaper invitation! Cut miniature diapers out of one large cloth diaper or white paper. Use a brightly colored felt tip marker or fabric paint to write out party details on the inside of each diaper, fold and secure with a diaper pin.

- Let a plain terry cloth bib be the adorable backdrop for a special invitation. Purchase bibs or sew your own out of terry cloth, add fabric painted information and you're done!

- Fold colored construction paper and reach for the scissors to fashion various shapes in keeping with your party — pacifiers, dolls, storks, bears, baby bottles, and tiny shoes are all perfect designs. Decorate the front with dainty satin ribbons and write party info on the inside.

- Purchase fine parchment paper to create tiny birth certificates. Use calligraphy or your best handwriting to fill in the blanks with party information.

- Pass out cigars ahead of time! Send chocolate or bubblegum cigars with a creamy white card attached. Have all your party details neatly written on the tag and use pink, blue, or yellow ribbon to secure it to the treat.

- Let your invitation float by writing it on a helium-filled balloon. Tie pink, blue, or yellow ribbons to the bottom of the balloon, tape the ends securely to the inside of a gift box, push your balloon inside, and tape the lid shut. This is one invitation that's sure to get their attention!

A Simple Sample:

You're Invited to a Baby Shower!

FOR:_____

DATE:_____ TIME:_____

PLACE:_____

_____

GIVEN BY:_____

RSVP:_____

(Write theme, colors, and any other special info here)

Decorations

Decorating Wizardry

With more and more baby showers being co-ed catered affairs, there's a new glitz to the traditional celebration. Even if you are not opting for the luxury of a caterer, your party can have that professional look by using your own creativity to change a "nice" party into a sensational one. Be imaginative and even a little daring when it comes to working out the small details of your party. Go for a spectacular centerpiece, for example, by putting your artistic side to work. Take a large watermelon and carve a baby carriage, attaching wheels created out of oranges, grapefruits, or melons. Fashion a contented infant out of apples and don't forget the bonnet!

Think of setting the perfect stage by decorating the room to the fullest. Amuse your guests by having them step into a room that has been magically transformed into a nursery or a toddler's bedroom. Use a crib or playpen to hold the gifts, and scatter toys, stuffed animals, dolls and games liberally around the room and on the floor. Don't forget the children's music playing in the background!

For that special group of sophisticated ladies, you might want to treat them to a totally different experience. Greet each guest with her own baby bottle (filled with champagne, of course!) Prepare the bottles by cutting a large hole in the nipple of each and sliding a plastic flex straw through the hole. Afterwards, the bottles can be sterilized and given to the new mother to start off her collection.

Turn to the chapter on decorating and table settings to get general ideas for your baby shower. With those as a basis, feel free to alter and modify any that appeal to you so that you can really "baby-proof" your own party.

Cuddly Party Ideas Fit For A Baby

Baby Sock Bouquet — make an unforgettable corsage to pin on the mother-to-be. Fashion the flower out of baby socks, ribbons, and diaper pins (SEE BABY SOCK FLOWERS.)

Baby Sock Centerpiece — create an imaginative floral arrangement out of a group of baby sock flowers. Depending on the colors of the socks you're using, you might also want to intersperse chocolate or fresh flowers throughout the spray.

Balloon Bounty — let cheerful helium balloons hug the ceiling, their colorful ribbons dangling high overhead. Plan to gather a few into a delightful floating centerpiece or tie individual ones to glasses or the backs of chairs. Send each guest home with a cheerful balloon reminder of an afternoon of fun.

Clown Fun — decorate with these guaranteed-to-make-you-smile old friends. Make clowns out of long balloons to scatter around the room. Let your centerpiece be magical. Purchase a few clown rag dolls to flop into a wicker basket, tie a bunch of helium balloons to the top and your adorable centerpiece is ready to go! Create clown faces out of scoops of ice cream. Fill in facial features with small gumdrops, add a whip cream ruffle for a collar and top with a sugar cone hat.

Dolls and Bears — everyone loves to snuggle up to these critters. Incorporate these favorites into your theme in an amusing centerpiece. Choose a colorful tin, basket, or miniature red wagon to carry your party table guests. Arrange the dolls and bears in different positions — lying down, sitting up, with one leg dangling over the side of the basket, peering out from under an arm, and flopping against each other. Follow through with the rest of the decor by propping them on bookshelves, letting them recline on chairs, and allowing them to stretch out on the floor throughout the room!

Storks — this popular bearer of "good news" belongs at a baby shower! Browse through party supply stores for darling paper storks to hang around the room or to be used in a creative centerpiece surrounded by matching paper plates at each table setting.

Toys and Trains — toys make a great decor for a baby shower. Let an express train wind through your buffet table or encircle a bunch of fresh flowers gathered in a vase in the center of your table. Spray wicker baskets a gleaming white and fill to overflowing with small baby items like rattles, bath sponges, and teething rings. Attach pink and white helium balloons to the sides of each basket and place along the buffet table.

Nursery Rhymes — reach into your fondest childhood memories for those unforgettable storybook and nursery rhyme characters and decorate accordingly. Let Mother Goose grace your buffet table while the cow jumps over the moon in your living room.

Fanciful Favors

Bubbles
Wind-up toys
Jacks
Puzzles
Yo-yo
Frizbee

For more party favor ideas, please see "Special Party Favors" (DECORATIONS AND TABLE SETTINGS.)

Diaper Invitation

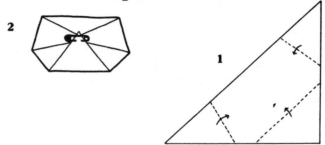

Instructions:

1. Cut a triangle of white paper or fabric, print shower information within dotted lines.
2. Fold all points into center and close with a decorative diaper pin.

Baby Sock Flowers

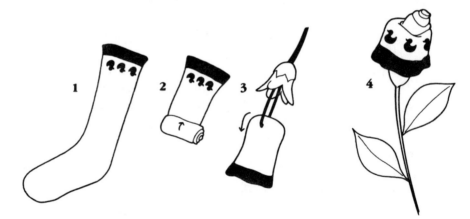

Supplies needed:

Plastic floral stems with green base (If only available with flowers simply remove flower.)

Thin green wire and floral tape

Pair of baby socks, makes 2 flowers

Instructions:

1. Lay each sock flat with top up.
2. Roll from toe up, stopping just above heel.
3. Pull top of sock down over the roll, run thin green wire through the bottom of roll pulling through floral base tucking the sock into it.
4. Pull top of the sock over the roll, attach flower by securing green wire to stem with floral tape.

140

BABY
SHOWER
THEMES
AND GIFTS

Chapter 15

BABY SHOWER THEMES

hether you are planning to create a theme for your shower or stay with the traditional format often depends on the mother-to-be. It's a good idea to check with her in the early stages of planning so that you can find out her preferences and needs. Along with the items she may need, it is important to determine if she would prefer to have a baby shower before or after her baby's arrival.

This will be the baby's first "social event" so it's up to you to make it everything it should be! Be creative and flexible in your planning and get set for a wonderful party.

Theme Ideas with That Special Touch

Miscellaneous Shower

This traditional shower is perfect for the first-time mother who hasn't started shopping for the pending arrival and still needs everything! You have total flexibility with this party — decide on a dessert party for ladies or a buffet dinner for couples and select your decorations accordingly. Guests can pool their resources for a group gift such as a playpen, car seat, or stroller, or choose to present the mother with individual presents selected from the multitude of adorable baby items currently on the market.

Time-of-day Shower

Since each guest is responsible for bringing a gift suitable for a designated time in a baby's day, this theme is a winner when it comes to assuring that there is a wide variety of gifts.

In planning your invitations, you may want to use the same one as you would for an Around-the-clock wedding shower (SEE WEDDING

INVITATIONS.) If you do decide on a clock invitation with the hands pointing to the guest's assigned time of day, be prepared to make a note of the activity that goes with that particular time. This helps minimize confusion since every baby has a different schedule. For example, if you have sent an invitation with noon showing on the face of the clock, write "mealtime" on the bottom or inside of the invitation.

Timely Gifts

Mealtime
    bottles and nipples
    quilted bottle covers
    bottle warmer
    feeding spoon
    cup
    food dishes
    high chair
    baby food grinder
    bibs
    warming dish
    portable table seat

Nap time
    blanket
    crib bumper pad
    crib mobile
    pajamas
    comforter
    stuffed animals
    wooden cradle

Playtime
    teething ring
    rattles
    plastic keys and beads
    crib gym or mobile
    playpen pad
    stuffed animals

Visiting time
    infant carrier
    car seat
    diaper bag
    disposable bottles and diapers
    a cute outfit
    lightweight blanket

car bottle warmer
changing mat
stroller

Bath time

baby shampoo
soap, oil, lotion, and powder
plastic baby tub
bath toys
washcloths and towels
receiving blankets
bathrobe
brush and comb

Bedtime

crib sheets
crib blankets
waterproof mattress pad
blanket sleeper
cuddly animals
portable intercom
night light
baby lamp

Nursery Shower

Help the excited parents get the most important room in the house ready and waiting for its new occupant by throwing a nursery shower. Carry out the theme by decorating your own party room as a grown-up nursery — pile all the gifts in a playpen in the center of the room, scatter toys along the buffet table, and tape cartoon characters around the room.

Since many of the items for a well-equipped nursery can be expensive, you may elect to purchase one collective gift and have each guest only bring only a small toy in addition.

Gifts for the Group to Give

crib
stroller
bassinet
playpen
changing table
chest of drawers
cradle
rocking chair

Small Gifts To Bring

crib toys
night light
mobile
shampoo, soap, lotion, and powder
nail clippers and file
diaper pail
diaper stacker
washcloths

Gift Basket Shower

By assigning a gift basket theme to each guest, this shower allows each celebrant to be as creative as she wishes. Assign each guest a specific theme or let them choose from a list tucked into your invitation. Each party-goer then gathers small items pertaining to her particular theme and arranges them in a basket or container of her choosing.

Bountiful Baskets

Basket for the bath — cheerfully stock a plastic tub with shampoo, soap, sponges and bath toys.

Diaper basket — stuff a hanging diaper stacker with all the necessities — diapers, diaper pins, wipes, baby ointment, and powder.

Nursery basket — choose a brightly colored diaper pail or basket to hold a baby blanket or changing pad, lotion, nail clippers, and a brush and comb set.

Feeding basket — pile bottles, nipples, pacifiers, teething rings, bottle brushes, and a selection of cute bibs into a pastel basket.

Traveling basket — use a baby carrier to cradle booties, a hat, and receiving blanket. You can also purchase as straw bassinet and line it with pretty fabric and a matching blanket.

Knapsack basket — select a cute cloth baby carrier such as a front wrap or a backpack-type. Add sun block, a hat, and booties, and you're set for the little traveler.

On-the-go basket — decide on a fun wicker tote to create a carrier the mother will not be able to live without. Stock it with disposable diapers, wipes, baby powder, and an extra bottle.

Hospital basket — shower the mother-to-be with a tote bag containing a toothbrush and toothpaste, hair brush, mirror, facial soap, lotion, slippers, and a new nightgown.

Coming-Out Shower

Introduce the new baby to society by hosting a Coming-out party a few weeks after the birth. The guests will get a chance to admire the adorable debutante and toast the new parents. Since the guests will know in advance whether they will be welcoming a boy or a girl, gift decisions concerning clothes and toys will be a breeze. It's nice to include such gift items as baby memory books and photo albums. As hostess you can also compile a scrapbook of the day the baby was born. Be sure to include the local newspaper's masthead with date, the daily horoscope, the weather, and clippings of sports, news, and fashion events. It is also interesting to toss in a few ads showing food prices, popular restaurants, and movies to see. The collection will be a fun first memory for the baby to browse through in the years to come.

Shower for a Second Baby

Since the mother's second or third child generally doesn't get the attention that the first one receives, a shower honoring this newborn will be greatly appreciated. Concentrate on either more personal gifts for the new child or items new to the market since most of the larger items, such as a stroller and playpen, will still be on-hand. If you know the sex of the expected baby, and it happens to be the opposite of the previous child, opt for clothes.

Shower for an Adopted Baby

Throw a "one-month birthday" party to share in the joy of an adopted child. Check with the mother to see what items she may still need. Chances are she will already have everything for the nursery, but additional clothes, toys and stuffed animals are always welcome. Include the father in the celebration by making it a co-ed brunch or dinner.

Shower for the Mother

The mother who is looking forward to the birth of her second or third child usually has all the baby items she needs. This is no reason not to throw her a baby shower. Just make it special by giving personal gifts to the mother-to-be. Consider having guests bring a variety of goodies to tuck into a hospital tote bag or present her with gift certificate for "the works" (manicure, pedicure, facial, massage, and beauty make-over.) Another thoughtful gift is concert, theater, or movie tickets along with a babysitting coupon good for that evening.

BABY SHOWER GAMES AND GIFTS

Chapter 16

BABY SHOWER
GAMES AND GIFTS

*E*ven though opening the presents will be one of the highlights of your party, you may want to add a special bit of sparkle to the entertainment by incorporating games into the planned festivities. A little friendly competition will get your guests laughing while acting as a smooth transition from the meal to the opening of the presents.

When selecting appropriate activities for your guests, try to stick to those which are not overly long or complicated. Keep in mind that if there are a lot of guests, there will be a lot of presents to open. No one likes to be rushed when opening gifts, so be sure to budget your time accordingly.

Consider starting the party off with "Diaper Pin Blooper" and following with a few other favorites that you feel will suit the number and interests of your guests. In calculating your prizes, be prepared with a back-up stock of goodies to settle those tie-breakers. If you're left with too many gifts toward the end of the games, feel free to award a consolation prize to the person who lost every game, had the fewest points in all the games, broke her pencil, or had the most original (but wrong) answers. If games just don't appeal to you, opt for the fun of a "A Baby Tee-shirt Painting Party," which is guaranteed to get everyone happily involved! Instead of games or a special group activity, you may simply wish to leave a generous amount of time for socializing, especially if close (and talkative!) friends are coming.

Baby Shower Games

Diaper Pin Blooper

This is a great starter activity. Pin a cute diaper pin on each guest as she comes through the door. As soon as the pin is in place, the guest is not allowed to use the word "baby" at any time during the shower. Whoever slips has to relinquish her pin to the guest who first catches the blooper. The guest who has accumulated the most diaper pins by the end of the party wins.

Who's Who

Ask each guest to bring along a baby picture of herself. Mount these "celebrity" photos on a bulletin board. Assign each a number by writing on the back lightly in pencil or attaching a numbered slip underneath each entry. Give each person a pencil and piece of paper and five minutes to unravel who's who. The one with an eye for faces and the most correct guesses wins a prize.

Take A Guess

Let your guests look into the future and make their own predictions with this game that only takes a small amount of preparation. Make a chart out of a large piece of colored cardboard. Across the top create four columns for the birthdate, sex, height, and weight. Write all the guests' names down the left-hand side. At the party, each participant has to guess what the final "outcome" will be. She then carefully records her predictions in the spaces following her name. Keep the chart until after the birth so that you can determine the winner. The one who comes closest to having all three estimates correct at the time of the birth will win. You can either award a prize or collect $1 from each guest to create a pot of money that the lucky winner will receive.

Diaper Mess

This is really more of a gag than a game but it gives everyone a good laugh. Purchase enough oversized white paper napkins to have one for each guest. Fold the napkins diagonally and place 4 or 5 plain chocolate M & M's in the center of each. Bring the pointed ends of the napkin diaper-fashion into the center and secure with tape. Pile all your diaper creations except one in a large bowl. Place the one set aside briefly in the microwave or oven, just long enough to melt the chocolate. When you're sure that diaper is sufficiently "gooey," add it to the others in the bowl. At your shower, let each guest choose her own diaper-shaped treat out of the bowl and get set for the laughs as only one gets stuck with a messy diaper!

How Big is Big?

By the time of your shower, the expectant mother should be beginning to look "big." But how big is she really? Test your guests' ability to judge her circumference by arranging the following game. Pass around a roll of toilet paper and instruct each person to take the amount she thinks it will take to fit around the mother-to-be's tummy. Once everyone has torn off their "measuring tape," use the remainder of the roll to really measure her and compare that strip with those of the guests. The "tailor" whose piece comes closest to the correct length wins the prize.

What's In the Bag?

Place a number of baby items in the bottom of a pillowcase, such as a pacifier, cotton balls, wipes, bottle, plastic keys, etc. Pass the pillowcase around, giving each person 30 seconds to one minute to feel what is in the bag before she passes it to the next player. After passing the bag, the guest must write down everything she can remember feeling in the bag. The winner of the prize is the one who remembers the most items correctly.

ABC Sentences

Make three-word sentences using the designated letters of the alphabet to start each word (ABC = All Babies Cry.) Use the form below to create sentences that a mother would be teaching her baby. The first one finished who has used all of the alphabet letters is awarded a prize and will be asked to read her sentences aloud. Be creative!!

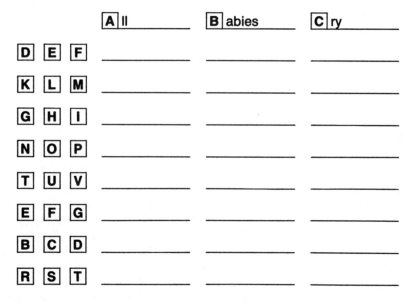

Scramble

The following words are all items that are used by a baby. The first person to unscramble the words correctly wins. If no one has unscrambled them all after 15 minutes, call "Time" and award the prize to the person with the most correct words. Rewrite this list or make up your own and photocopy individual lists for your guests.

1. Gwins _____
2. Pealynp _____
3. Lenkbat _____
4. Retalt _____
5. Paried _____
6. Tolbet _____
7. Blomie _____
8. Restlorl _____
9. Bric _____
10. Sabitnes _____

Scramble Answers:
1. Swing
2. Playpen
3. Blanket
4. Rattle
5. Diaper
6. Bottle
7. Mobile
8. Stroller
9. Crib
10. Bassinet

Picture This

Here's a lively game based on the popular "Pictionary" that's a great way to get everyone moving. Divide the group into two teams (SEE DIRECTIONS BELOW) and have each team select an "artist," who will be responsible for drawing a picture while the rest of the team will try to guess what it means. The hostess prepares for the game by writing down sentences on slips of paper describing activities that the new mother will be doing with her baby. Choose any of the following activities or make up your own: mixing formula, burping the baby, going for a walk, changing the baby, washing diapers, and going to the Pediatrician. Place all the slips in a large hat. At the start of each round, the two team artists draw a slip out of the hat. On the word "Go!" they open their slips, read their sentence, and rush to their team to begin drawing the activity written on their slip. The first team to guess correctly what their team sketcher has drawn, wins that round. The losers of the round become spectators. After the first round, the winners are again divided into two separate groups to begin a second round. The new groups select different team artists and the game begins again. If you have enough guests, the winners of the second round can be divided into another two teams for the third and final round of competition. The winners of this play-off round are then each given a prize. Adjust the number of rounds according to the number of guests playing. A small group will have only two rounds, a larger probably four. If any memorable sketches are accidently produced, present them to the guest of honor as a momento of a great party!

How to Divide the Teams (For 24 Guests)

1. Have both pink and pale blue construction paper ready. Cut out 12 pink and 12 white 1 x 4" slips and separate into two piles.

2. On three of the pink and three of the blue slips write: "GIRL, PACIFIER."

3. On three of the white and three of the pink slips write: "GIRL, BOTTLE."

4. On three of the white and three of the pink slips write: "BOY, PACIFIER."

5. On three of the white and three of the pink slips write: "BOY, BOTTLE."

6. Everybody draws one of these slips from a hat and two teams, one pink and one blue are formed.

7. At the end of round 1, either the pink or the blue team wins. At this point the winning team redivides into two new teams: GIRLS vs BOYS.

8. The third and final round will be played between the PACIFIERS and the BOTTLES.

A Baby Tee-Shirt Painting Party

Have fun with something entirely different! Instead of games, have your guests spend the afternoon painting adorable baby tee-shirts. Because the tee-shirts created are then presented to the expectant mother, this is a perfect choice for the shower where gifts are not expected.

Purchase plain, white tee-shirts in various sizes ranging from 2 months to toddler 2, along with a nice selection of fabric paints. Give each person a tee-shirt to paint and let them create the design and choose the colors themselves. For a slightly different twist, you can elect to make it a competition with the mother-to-be acting as judge. You can give a small favor to practically every budding Picasso present by awarding prizes for a wide variety of categories — the prettiest, the most colorful, the funniest, the most creative, etc. These delightful creations will be a welcomed addition to the baby's wardrobe, as well as serving as a "walking" reminder of a very special day.

Opening Gifts

Since everyone looks forward to the opening of the gifts, make sure that it has the spotlight it deserves. Set a comfortable chair in a location that will be visible to all the well-wishers. Assign someone to keep track of the presents and their thoughtful givers so that there will be a written record for the mother to refer to when writing thank-you notes.

If you are in search of a creative alternative to store-bought items, have people consider giving a unique but thoughtful gift. Create coupons which can be redeemed for babysitting, shopping, cooking a meal, cleaning the house, or any other activity you can think of to make the months ahead just a little easier. Another thoughtful alternative is to ask each guest to bring a favorite dish ready to store in the freezer until after the baby is born. By stocking the family freezer ahead of time, both mother and father will be spared a good deal of exhausting shopping and cooking. Be sure that each cook has put both her name and the name of the dish securely on the outside so that the couple is not in for too many surprises! This is a deliciously different idea that is guaranteed to elicit an on-going round of applause from the soon-to-be-worn-out young couple.

Index

Index (continued)

— Notes —

— Notes —

— Notes —

— Notes —

— Notes —

— Notes —

— Notes —

— Notes —

— Notes —

— Notes —

Order Form

Additional copies of "Showers" and our book "Planning a Wedding to Remember" can be purchased through major book stores, bridal salons and gift stores. If not available in your area use the order form provided.

Send to:

Name _____

Street Address _____

_____

City _____

State _____ Zip _____

Day Phone (_____) _____

Please send me the following:

_____ "Showers" – $8.95 each $ _____

Number of copies

_____ "Planning a Wedding to Remember" – $15.95 each $ _____

Number of copies

(CA add 7.75% Sales Tax) $ _____

Add $1.50 for the book and $1.00 for each additional book $ _____

TOTAL ORDER $ _____

☐ Send a free catalog of The Beverly Clark Collection of wedding accessories.

Send check or money order to: Beverly Clark Collection

6385 B. Rose Ln.

Carpenteria, CA 93013

Credit Card Orders
Call (800) 888-6866 or (805) 566-1425

Between 8:30 am and 5:00 pm (west coast time) weekdays.

Method of payment (check one)
    ☐ check or money order (sorry no C.O.D.'s)
    ☐ Visa
    ☐ MasterCard

Issuing Bank _____ Exp. Date _____

Credit Card Number

Signature _____

Order Form

Additional copies of "Showers" and our book "Planning a Wedding to Remember" can be purchased through major book stores, bridal salons and gift stores. If not available in your area use the order form provided.

Send to:

Name _____

Street Address _____

_____

City _____

State _____ Zip _____

Day Phone (_____) _____

Please send me the following:

_____ "Showers" – $8.95 each $ _____
Number of copies

_____ "Planning a Wedding to Remember" – $15.95 each $ _____
Number of copies

(CA add 7.75% Sales Tax) $ _____

Add $1.50 for the book and $1.00 for each additional book $ _____

TOTAL ORDER $ _____

☐ Send a free catalog of The Beverly Clark Collection of wedding accessories.

Send check or money order to: Beverly Clark Collection
6385 B. Rose Ln.
Carpenteria, CA 93013

Credit Card Orders
Call (800) 888-6866 or (805) 566-1425

Between 8:30 am and 5:00 pm (west coast time) weekdays.

Method of payment (check one)
☐ check or money order (sorry no C.O.D.'s)
☐ Visa
☐ MasterCard

Issuing Bank _____ Exp. Date _____

Credit Card Number

Signature _____

OUR CALL
to
FAITHFULNESS

THE VOICE AND LEGACY OF
DON WILDMON

PRINTED IN THE UNITED STATES OF AMERICA

ISBN 978-1-5136-1549-3

American Family Publishing
A division of American Family Association
107 Parkgate Drive
Tupelo, MS 38801

www.afa.net

Cover design by Canada Burkhalter

Editorial contributions by Randall Murphree, Rusty Benson, Debbie Fischer, and Ed Vitagliano

Project oversight by Buddy Smith

TABLE OF CONTENTS

APPENDIX

PREFACE

"I'm Don. I am who I am. I am what you see," said Don Wildmon, founder of AFA, father of four, grandfather of six, and great-grandfather of three.

Those closest to him might say he's a kid at heart. He says he has the mind of a child.

Either way, he reasons, "Kids always have fun. You might as well have fun. After all, it takes fewer muscles to laugh than to frown."

This is a side to Wildmon not many see outside the home and office. Why?

"Because it's the only two places I go," Wildmon said without cracking a smile. His dry sense of humor and quick wit are part of who he is, and it doesn't matter to him what others think.

"It matters what I think of me, and it matters what God thinks of me," he explained. "I'm not very good at verbalizing my Christian faith. I try to show what I believe in my actions."

One belief Wildmon hopes to communicate to his grandchildren and great-grandchildren is a lesson he has learned time and time again during his years of ministry: "Life is not always easy, and the goal in life is not happiness but holiness."

It's not about having a holier-than-thou attitude, but rather a desire to do the best for the Lord.

"Life is not going to be on mountaintops all the time. You're going to fail a whole lot more than you succeed, but you must not let failure be fatal," he added.

While the world defines success in terms of big houses, fancy cars, and loads of money, Wildmon finds assurance in knowing he belongs to God. "I'm God's child and out of that flows everything else."

INTRODUCTION

He has always said a lot in just a few words. Many times his actions really did speak louder than his words. But then again, at other times, people felt like he said too much … *and* did too much. Little or a lot, his words and his ways were and will always be of great value to me. After all, he is Dad.

This collection of columns written by my dad, Don Wildmon, originally appeared in *AFA Journal*, the 28-page national publication of American Family Association that now reaches about 150,000 subscribers each month.

His earliest writings were published in the *Newsletter of the National Federation for Decency*, an 8½ x 14-inch sheet printed on two sides. Over time, the newsletter turned into *NFD Informer* and eventually *AFA Journal*.

One of my dad's first newsletters published in the late 1970s included a personal plea for support to continue the work that resulted from his family and his church observing "Turn The Television Off Week." The campaign became a national effort … and then a national ministry that has been influencing the culture for the glory of God since 1977.

Over the years, Dad has written hundreds of monthly columns on various topics related to culture issues, personal living, and Christian activism. The ones we've collected here are what we at American Family Association consider to be some of the best of his timeless wisdom and insight.

In my opinion, they are worth reading now, and again … and again. This is his voice and his legacy. May he inspire and challenge you like he has me.

Tim Wildmon

The Enemy Is Us

APRIL 1986

The comic strip character Pogo once had a saying: "We have met the enemy, and he is us."

Truly, the same could be said for the Christian community. We are our worst enemy. There is a war going on unlike any war we have ever fought in our society. It is a spiritual war, a war for the hearts and minds of mankind. Many Christians are either unaware or indifferent to that war. The struggle will determine whether the Christian view of man will continue to serve as the foundation for our society.

I have no easy cliché answers to the problem, but I think that after nearly 10 years I have some perspective that might not be seen (and sometimes not shared) by others. We have neglected the cross, the Christian symbol of suffering and redemption. We have attempted to make Christianity compatible with any and all other religions – secularism, materialism, humanism, etc. We have attempted to make Christianity something it is not – a vehicle to worldly success, worldly contentment, worldly happiness.

"Whoever wants to be my disciple must deny themselves and take up their cross daily and follow me" (Luke 9:23). It is as valid today as it was 2,000 years ago.

There is a move – a massive move – afoot in our society to eliminate the influence of Christianity. It is fueled not only by people who are apathetic to the Christian faith, but by many who are hostile to the Christian faith.

1

Even so, our own worst enemy is us. We have been negligent in our thinking. We have, too much, bought the old clichés.

You can't legislate morality. Yet every law on the books is a legislation of morality.

You should not mix politics and religion. And we haven't. Keeping our Christian faith private, we have allowed a situation where 1.5 million unborn babies have their lives snuffed out each year.

You should keep religion out of the schools, even as it provides a moral base. And we have. But those who would eliminate the influence of Christianity have not. They have pushed their religion of secularism, materialism, and humanism into the schools.

According to Dr. Paul Vitz of New York University, those responsible for our textbooks "appear to have a deep-seated fear of any form of active contemporary Christianity." In the process, while complaining about censorship, they have censored Christianity to the point that in most children's textbooks it doesn't exist at worst, or it doesn't matter at best. It plays no role, gets no notice, from those who prepare the textbooks for our school children. We have allowed others, who don't share our view of life and are openly hostile to it, to do our most serious thinking.

We have, nearly without a whimper, accepted television entertainment and movies that continually mock and belittle Christianity and Christians. We have allowed radio to air vulgar and violent music that Christians two decades ago would never have tolerated.

Our own worst enemy is us. There is no glory in fighting a war, even a spiritual war. There is only suffering and pain.

2

Does the Christian community have enough of what it takes to turn this tide, to stop the decay of Western civilization?

Do we have enough Christians who are willing to pay the price, to make the sacrifices necessary so that they can provide the leadership needed in their pulpits, in their homes, and in their communities?

The answer to that question remains to be seen. And in the balance hangs the future of Western civilization.

Shall We Have Respectability at the Loss of Responsibility?

JANUARY 1987

Back when I had the privilege of serving a local church as pastor, I would preach the same sermon two or three times over a period of months or years. The reason? Some things need to be said more than once, just as some things should never be said the first time.

I would hate to count the times I have said in this column, and in appearances all over this great country, that we are in the midst of a spiritual war. But that is precisely the situation.

At stake in this spiritual war is the very foundation, not only of our country but of the whole of Western civilization. The progress we have made, the freedoms we have enjoyed these past two centuries, have come primarily because our society was founded on the Christian view of man.

There is an intentional, powerful effort currently being made to change the base of that foundation, to rid it of Christian influence, and to replace that base with a secular, materialist, humanistic view of man.

Three hundred years from now when historians write about the current era in which we live, they will refer to this spiritual war as being the most important struggle the organized church has faced since Constantine. I am sure of that. What I am not sure of is how they will report the outcome.

The organized church has spent far too much time and placed far too much importance on buildings and budgets and far too little time informing and leading its people in facing this spiritual war. Too much of our activity, at the local church level and at the denominational level, has been inward. "Whoever finds their life will lose it, and whoever loses their life for my sake will find it" (Matthew 10:39). That is as true for the organized church as it is for individuals.

Let me paraphrase some other words of Jesus found in Mark 8:36: What shall it profit a church if it builds the largest and finest buildings, fills them with people, and raises great sums of money, while its members lose their souls?

I am not saying that buildings and budgets aren't important; they are. But I am saying that there is something far more important.

The increase in crime, breakdown of families, and increases in divorce, abortion, pornography, etc., are not simply separate areas of concern. They are all interrelated symptoms of the spiritual war being waged.

At the very heart of the Christian gospel is a cross – the symbol of suffering and sacrifice, of hurt and pain and humiliation and rejection.

I want no part of a Christian message that does not call me to involvement, requires of me no sacrifice, takes from me no comfort, requires of me less than my best.

The duty of a Christian is to be faithful, not popular or successful.

I hope, for our Lord's sake and the sake of those who come after us, that those of us who bear Christ's name will not shirk our responsibility for the sake of respectability.

If Christ will use this repentant sinner as a soldier in this spiritual war, I will count it the highest honor I could receive.

Actions Have Consequences

APRIL 1993

When I was 18 years of age and prepared to leave home to go to college, I had never lived in a house that had a lock on a door or window. A lock simply wasn't needed. That is not to say that people did not steal in those days. It is to say that the commonly accepted, widely practiced underlying belief was that stealing was wrong.

That moral was taught in our homes, in our churches, and in our schools. Society as a whole viewed moral behavior as being an important element in life. The combined pressure from society's institutions managed to keep the publicly accepted morality based on Judeo-Christian values. Back in those days, our streets were safer, our homes and families more solid, our crime less violent, and our moral standards higher. Sure, there were wrongs. But there was also a norm that could be used to address those wrongs.

Then came television and, unfortunately, a change in the attitude and values of those in the entertainment media. The old prohibitions were removed. The *Playboy* philosophy came to be the norm in Hollywood and at network headquarters in New York. The old attitudes based on 20 centuries of practice were scorned.

Before long, those who held contempt for the old values gathered new friends. They were small in number, but they were in very influential places. They held important positions in education, the media, the legal system, and other areas of influence.

For nearly 30 years now, our entertainment media and their friends have scorned, ridiculed, belittled, and bashed those old values. And now our society is beginning to reap what they have sown. New values of freedom without responsibility, immediate gratification, materialism, and sexual freedom have brought us an ever increasing amount of crime, drug use, family breakdown, AIDS, etc. The list goes on and on.

Actions have consequences. For every action there is a reaction. We do indeed reap what we sow. We are at a very critical point in our history. Will we totally abandon the values that have made our nation strong for 200 years? Will we continue to pursue our current path and follow the *Playboy* philosophy until we reach our ruin?

The answer to that question depends on what those of us who still believe in the old values do – or fail to do. We can draw back when criticized. We can remain in our shell and refuse to get involved.

Or we can do what those who went before us did: We can work to implant and maintain those old time-proven values as the norm. The decision is ours. And resting on that decision is the future of our nation.

Would the Real Jesus Please Stand Up?

SEPTEMBER 1993

I have met these people, many of them during the past 16 years. I know when it is coming. I can hear it (in the tone of their voices and in their suggestions on how I should act in order to be a good Christian). They all make about the same points. Here is a general outline of their suggestions.

1. Jesus didn't criticize people; therefore, I should not criticize those who are responsible for filth on television or who produce and distribute pornography.

2. Jesus didn't condemn anyone; He loved them. They usually point to the woman caught in the act of adultery on this one. They even quote Scripture: "Neither do I condemn thee: go and sin no more," (John 8:11, KJV).

3. Jesus lived His life so that people respected Him and sought to follow Him. As Christians, we need to live our lives in a similar manner. That means that we don't disagree with anyone; rather, we try to convince him or her by our actions and not our words.

4. Jesus made friends with everyone. He accepted everyone. He was even a friend to those with whom He disagreed. He didn't turn them off simply because they disagreed with Him.

As a young minister, I read a story told by J. Wallace Hamilton, a preacher of note who died in 1968. According to the story, it seems that a not-too-dignified but somewhat successful preacher was preaching at a chapel service at a large and respected university.

Now this preacher was not a good public relations person. He was somewhat unreserved and preached what many would call a straightforward, perhaps even blunt, sermon. I'm sure that you have heard that kind. He called sin ... sin. Then laid out the plan of salvation.

He just wasn't a very tactful preacher; his bluntness offended some who were present.

Following his sermon, he was met at the back by one of the professors. Calling the preacher aside, the professor told him that he had preached a good sermon but that if he would change it just a little, not be so straightforward, that he could do so much more good.

"You know," the professor said, "if you will search the Scriptures you will find that Jesus was the most loving, non-condemning, forgiving, helpful person who ever lived. I'm simply suggesting that you make your sermons as tactful as Jesus made his. It would really help your ministry."

The preacher thought for a moment. "You think I need to be more tactful?" he asked.

"I think it would be a big help to your ministry," said the professor.

"Was Jesus a tactful person?" the preacher asked.

"The most tactful person who ever lived," responded the professor.

The preacher thought a little more then spoke: "Professor, please answer a question for me. If Jesus was the most tactful person who ever lived, how did He manage to get Himself crucified?"

The professor did not answer the question.

The Set of the Soul Decides Its Goal

JUNE 1994

One of my favorite poems is this one written by Ella Wheeler
Wilcox:

> *One ship drives east and another drives west*
> *With the selfsame winds that blow;*
> *'Tis the set of the sails*
> *And not the gales*
> *That tells them the way to go.*
>
> *Like the winds of the sea are the winds of fate,*
> *As we voyage along through life;*
> *'Tis the set of the soul*
> *That decides its goal*
> *And not the calm or the strife.*

I have often wondered why there are so many individuals
who frequent our churches but who are unconcerned about
the spiritual and cultural war being waged in our society.
With so much at stake, it should be that every person who
calls himself a Christian should be active and involved
in trying to turn back the tide of immorality that seeks to
engulf us.

We leaders in the church are responsible for the apathy
that exists in our midst. For years, our emphasis has been
almost totally on trying to get people to come to church
instead of be the church. We have been more concerned with
the building than with being. We have left the impression to

those who come to our sanctuaries that if they will attend worship with some degree of regularity, give some part of their income, and assume some small role in keeping the institution (both locally and denominationally) going, then they have fulfilled their "requirements" of citizenship in the Kingdom.

Baptist preacher Vance Havner once said that the worst thing that happened to the church was when Constantine made it the religion of the Roman Empire. It gave Christianity respectability. And most of us want respectability more than we want responsibility. We don't really expect our faith to require much of us, nor to cost us much of our comfort. We expect little or no sacrifice.

> Like the winds of the sea are the winds of fate,
> As we voyage along through life;
> 'Tis the set of a soul
> That decides its goal
> And not the calm or the strife.

"Enter through the narrow gate. For wide is the gate and broad is the road that leads to destruction, and many enter through it," said Jesus. "But small is the gate and narrow the road that leads to life, and only a few find it" (Matthew 7:13–14).

There are those who seek the comfort of the sanctuary, and there are those who seek the cause of the Savior. They are not the same.

Why? They differ because of the set of the soul.

14

Three Drunks at a Ball Game

I went to a college football game recently. I used to go quite often but have not attended many games lately. One of the reasons I haven't gone is that over the past few years it has been my luck to sit near some drunk whose foul mouth and behavior ruin the game for everyone. Who cares about giving $25 to spend three hours being offended by some drunk?

But this was a big game – Mississippi State and Ole Miss – and my daughter, son-in-law, and son wanted me to go. So my wife Lynda and I loaded up and went along. It will probably be the last one I will go to for a long, long time. You guessed it. One row up behind us were three drunks. For three hours we, and all those around us, were bombarded with the most profane, vulgar, senseless language and behavior imaginable.

I pondered what to do about the situation. I thought about speaking with the drunks and asking them to act decently. But I have never had any success with drunks whose intent is to be as profane as they can be. I must confess, and ask the Lord's forgiveness, that I also thought about turning around and swinging as hard as I could with my fist hoping it would meet the mark. But I knew that was not the answer.

When the drunks got into a near fight with another man sitting next to Lynda, I was wondering what the papers would say the next day should a fight break out. The man explained to the drunks that his first-grade grandson was sitting with him and asked them to tone it down. I knew that I was not going to let the grandfather who was trying to reason with three drunks fight them alone. I could already see the headlines: "AFA president involved in brawl at football game." The media would have had a field day with that.

What did I do? I simply endured it. After a long period of thinking of all my options, I decided that was probably the best – to endure it. I did a lot of thinking while listening to the drunks. I thought about how much the morals in our society have declined. Having gone to many ball games as a kid, I did see some drunks, but I never witnessed the kind of behavior that is commonplace at games today.

I thought about how the movies have changed, the television programs have changed, and the music has changed. I thought about the increase in crime, the explosion of drug and alcohol use, the increase in the number of abortions, etc.

I also thought about how the blame for this decline must be shared by many. Among them are parents who don't care. Bleeding-heart liberals who say that society is to blame. Politicians who are willing to give away billions of tax dollars in "social" programs just to get re-elected, programs that help sink people into more irresponsibility. A national media, both news and entertainment, dominated by people pushing a secular, liberal philosophy. An education system controlled by the National Education Association, which is far more interested in a political agenda than educating children.

And, yes – as much as I hate to say it – churches and individual Christians who have remained silent, who have withdrawn their voices from the public arena, or who (in the name of "rights" or "freedom") have joined with those helping destroy the moral fabric of our nation.

Leaving the game, I felt dirty all over. But I left realizing anew just how important the work of AFA is and how far we have to go to restore a basic common decency in our society.

Like Solomon, I ask God for wisdom to know what to do. … And the courage to do it.

The Greatest Gift You Can Give Your Children

MARCH 1997

The smartest thing I ever did in my life was to make a decision to follow Jesus Christ. I remember making that decision when I was about nine years of age. I renewed it when I was about 18. The decision to follow Christ has made all the difference in my life.

Recently I celebrated my 59th birthday. As I look back, I see how good God has been to me. Not only that, but I see a glimmer of the goodness of God. I can't understand his total love for His children because I don't have that ability.

But I do understand a small bit of it.

I shudder to think what my life would be like had I not decided to follow Christ. I won't go into all the details, but let me just say it would be vastly different.

Of course, the best thing I had going for me was that I was born into a home headed by a Christian mother and father. How fortunate I was! And they, when growing up, had that same advantage. I confess with the writer of Proverbs:

"For I too was a son to my father. ... [H]e taught me, and he said to me, 'Take hold of my words with all your heart ...'" (Proverbs 4:3–4). I did hold on to the words of my parents, which were a reflection of God's words. I have never regretted it.

Several years ago, I preached a funeral sermon. At the gravesite, I was approached by a person I did not know and was asked if my grandfather was John Wildmon. When I said yes, the stranger said my grandfather was one of the finest persons he ever knew. Imagine that! A grandfather I never met made a decision years before I was born that affected my life dramatically. That's the way life works.

My Grandfather Wildmon died before I was born. I hardly knew my Grandmother Wildmon, as she died when I was relatively young, and we hardly ever visited with her because of the distance involved.

My mother lost her mother when she was seven and her father when she was 12. My mother devoted her life to her family – children and grandchildren. I was grown before I realized why she put so much emphasis on family. It was simply because she never had one.

Our society is becoming increasingly more pagan. Children today will not be able to avoid facing that pagan society. Each one will make decisions as to what he wants to do with his life, how he will live and react to the hedonistic culture around him.

I am convinced that the finest gift parents can give to their children is to raise them in a Christian home. Every other gift comes in a distant second – not even close.

I hope your children and grandchildren have that advantage.

Trust and Obey,
for There's No Other Way

The Christian life is a marathon, not a 100-yard dash. We need to keep that truth in mind in today's world. Our culture is so absorbed with winning, with instant gratification, and with shortcuts that we have a tendency to apply those same standards to our relationship with God.

Paul spoke to this situation in the fourth chapter of Second Timothy.

For the time will come when people will not put up with sound doctrine. Instead, to suit their own desires, they will gather around them a great number of teachers to say what their itching ears want to hear. They will turn their ears away from the truth and turn aside to myths. But you, keep your head in all situations, endure hardship, do the work of an evangelist, discharge all the duties of your ministry.

For I am already being poured out like a drink offering, and the time for my departure is near. I have fought the good fight, I have finished the race, I have kept the faith. Now there is in store for me the crown of righteousness, which the Lord, the righteous Judge, will award to me on that day – and not only to me, but also to all who have longed for his appearing (3–8).

Paul didn't say he had won. Paul did say he had kept the faith. He stayed faithful in the midst of the same situations in which we find ourselves.

God does not require of us that which we cannot do. Oftentimes we have no control over the outcome of the battle. But we have complete control over our response to the battle. God does not require that we be successful. He only asks that we be faithful. That we can do.

So, if it often looks like we are losing, just remember that the battle belongs to the Lord. Our duty is to remain in it and stay faithful.

A few verses further into Paul's letter to Timothy, he mentions Demas. Three times in Scripture Paul speaks of Demas. In his letter to Philemon, he refers to Demas as his fellow worker. In Colossians, he simply refers to Demas without comment.

Finally, in his second letter to Timothy (4:10), Paul writes: "[F]or Demas, because he loved this world, has deserted me. …"

Just remember, as we continue in the battle, that our Christian faith is a marathon, not a 100-yard dash.

That's What Christians Do Now

AUGUST 1999

In 1973, the Supreme Court said it was OK to kill unborn babies. Since then, we have killed more than the entire population of Canada. And it continues. A woman's choice? Half of those who have died in their mothers' wombs have been females. They didn't have a choice. It is called abortion.

Me? I go to church, the minister preaches, I go home. That's what Christians do now.

First it was in dingy, dirty theaters. Then convenience stores. Then grocery stores. Then on television. Now it is in the homes of millions via the Internet. It is called pornography.

Me? I go to church, the minister preaches, I go home. That's what Christians do now.

They called it no-fault. Why should we blame anyone when something so tragic happens? Haven't they already suffered enough? Half of the marriages in America end this way. The children suffered. The family broke down. It is called divorce.

Me? I go to church, the minister preaches, I go home. That's what Christians do now.

At one time it was a perversion. We kept it secret. We secured help and hope for those who practiced it. Now it is praised. We have parades celebrating it, and elected officials give it their blessing. Now it is endowed with special privileges and protected by special laws. Even some Christian leaders and denominations praise it. It is called homosexuality.

Me? I go to church, the minister preaches, I go home. That's what Christians do now.

It used to be an embarrassment. A shame. Now a third of all births are to mothers who aren't married. Two-thirds of all African-American children are born into a home without a father. The state usually pays the tab. That is why we pay our taxes, so that the government can take the place of parents. After all, government bureaucrats know much better how to raise children than parents do. It is called illegitimacy.

Me? I go to church, the minister preaches, I go home. That's what Christians do now.

At one time it was wrong. But then the state decided to legalize it, promote it, and tax it. It has ripped apart families and destroyed lives. But just look at all the money the state has raised. No longer do we have to teach our children to study and work hard. Now we teach them they can get something for nothing. We spend millions encouraging people to join the fun and excitement. Just look at the big sums that people are winning. They will never have to work again! It is called gambling.

Me? I go to church, the minister preaches, I go home. That's what Christians do now.

Not long ago, Christians were the good guys. But now any positive image of Christians in movies or on TV is gone. We are now depicted as the bad guys – greedy, narrow-minded hypocrites. The teacher can't have a Bible on his desk, but he can have an issue of *Playboy*. We don't have Christmas and Easter holidays – just winter break and spring break. We can't pray in school but can use foul language. It's called being tolerant.

Me? I go to church, the minister preaches, I go home. That's what Christians do now.

Yes, all these things came to pass within 30 years. Where were the Christians? Why, they were in church. All these things are for someone else to deal with. Times have changed. Involvement has been replaced with apathy.

But don't blame me. I didn't do anything. I go to church, the minister preaches, I go home. That's what Christians do now.

Faithfulness in the Bean Field

JANUARY 2000

As we enter a new year, a new decade, a new century, and a new millennium, I want to share a simple biblical principle with you.

Sometimes God asks us to be obedient and persevere in difficult circumstances even when victory seems very far away. It's called faithfulness.

"Let us not become weary in doing good, for at the proper time we will reap a harvest if we do not give up" (Galatians 6:9). Those, of course, are Paul's words to the churches of Galatia.

Let us make those words our motto. We have much work to do for the Lord.

Even as many church leaders encourage us to abandon our heritage and scriptural wisdom, let us continue to stand for truth, to do what we can to turn the tide of sin engulfing our society.

The Scripture tells us about some of the men who stood with David when the enemies of God's people pressed in all around them. Those men are called David's "mighty warriors."

We are told very little about them, but what we are told should greatly encourage us.

The first man mentioned in 2 Samuel 23:8–12 is Josheb-Basshebeth, who fought against Israel's enemy and killed 800 men at one time. Josheb was faithful even though the odds appeared stacked against him.

The second of the "mighty warriors" was Eleazar. He stood with David in defiance of the Philistines even when "the Israelites retreated." Eleazar was faithful even though he stood nearly alone against those who would enslave the people of God.

In battle, this man of God "stood his ground and struck down the Philistines till his hand grew tired and froze to the sword." Have you ever felt that way?

Have you ever been so spiritually weary and worn that it would have felt so good just to drop that sword, or that plow, or that pulpit, or that marriage, or those kids for a while?

Eleazar remained faithful in the midst of that kind of weariness. And yet the Bible tells us that because he did not quit, "the Lord brought about a great victory that day."

Finally, there was Shammah, who also found himself abandoned by the other warriors of Israel as the Philistines approached to do battle. Now Shammah found himself in "a field full of lentils." Literally, this man was standing in a bean field. We are not told that it held any strategic significance or military value.

But that bean field is where Shammah found himself staring across at the Philistines.

That was where the fight was, and that was where this mighty man of God stood fast.

Shammah "took his stand in the middle of the field. He defended it and struck the Philistines down, and the Lord brought about a great victory."

Sometimes God places us in a situation in which we ask, "Why should I fight this fight? It's just not worth it!" But God knows the value of the bean field, even if we don't.

He calls us to stand fast anyway.

As we come to this point in history, I want to take this opportunity to thank each of you who have stood with us, some of you for many years.

Let us keep on keeping on. It is not always within our ability to be successful. But it is always within our ability to be faithful.

Light Through the Clouds

APRIL 2000

A dark cloud has descended on America. Once the land of freedom and responsibility, once a culture guided by a Judeo-Christian heritage, once a land where righteousness was exalted, America has been shrouded by a dark cloud. This cloud has left us unable to tell right from wrong.

Indeed it has caused us to call wrong, right.

In pursuit of what is politically correct, tolerant, and diverse, we have not only permitted but promoted a way of life that – should we continue to follow it – will ultimately destroy this grand experiment we call America.

We have lost sight of who we are, from whence we came, and where we are headed.

Our leaders – both secular and religious – define morality only in corporate terms, not in individual terms. Only society can do wrong, not the individual. Unless, of course, the individual happens to follow the teachings of Holy Writ. Then he is condemned and radicalized.

This dark cloud has left us stumbling to and fro, hunting for a way through the darkness without falling. But falling we are. A seven-year-old boy kills an innocent six-year-old girl at his school. The media blames the object – a gun – while admitting that his home life was a mockery but never connecting the quality of his home life to his actions, nor mentioning the need for a solid stable family with a loving and present father and mother.

Because of this dark cloud, our children are being murdered in Littleton, Pearl, Edinboro, Paducah, Jonesboro, and Springfield. They are being dragged into a life of hopeless despair on the streets of our cities where crime flourishes and drugs flow. Our response is to take more money from the homes where it is needed, where a real difference could be made, and send it to Washington where someone seeking votes wants to use it to replace real love.

So many of our churches are seeking success defined by society – bigger being better.

They have so often forgotten that Christianity is, at its core, one beggar telling another beggar where to find bread to feed his hunger.

So many in positions of influence are pushing for society to abandon those values that have lifted and guided Western civilization for the past 2,000 years. They seek to redefine right and wrong, remove God from society, and, thus, make sin obsolete.

They are the blind leading the blind, and many are blindly following.

There is a way to lift this cloud of darkness; there is a light to show us the way. "I am the light of the world," He said. "Whoever follows me will never walk in darkness, but will have the light of life" (John 8:12).

Whether the cloud of darkness will be lifted, I do not know. One thing, however, I do know. For individuals who choose, there is a light to lead us out of the darkness. We need to do the best we can in following that light and sharing Him with others.

This Is a Story About a Lifesaving Station – I Think

JANUARY 2001

Once upon a time there was a region on the Northeast Coast that was very dangerous for ships because of many hidden shoals and rocks and sudden unexpected storms. Ships were being sunk, lives were being lost, families broken apart, and many sailors injured for life because of shipwrecks in the area.

One day a concerned individual came up with an idea. Why not build a lifesaving station in the area? Its purpose would be to warn ships in advance and to rescue those who were wrecked. He shared his idea with a few friends and neighbors, and before long they had built a lifesaving station, bought boats and buoys, and even built a lighthouse.

It was such a good idea that many people joined in. Many lives were saved, many families held together, and many injuries avoided. For years, people were proud of the good that the lifesaving station did.

Over a period of time the lifesaving station became a central part of their lives. They held fellowship suppers, social events, and special meetings at the building. Then one day some of the members of the lifesaving station decided that the old building needed repair. The furniture was worn, the seats and facilities uncomfortable. So the people decided to build a new lifesaving station.

When it was completed, they had the largest, most beautiful, most functional lifesaving building around. They increased the number of activities in the building. They held all kinds of social events. More and more people became a part of their lifesaving fellowship.

But a strange thing was happening. Fewer and fewer people were willing to go out and warn the ships, and even fewer were willing to go out in a storm to rescue sailors from a wrecked ship. The activities at the lifesaving station took all their time. They just didn't have time to save lives. So they decided to hire others – professional lifesavers – to do the job for them. They could support the lifesaving station without becoming directly involved in the difficult, unpleasant job of saving lives.

Several years later the members of the lifesaving station decided that the lifesaving activities were taking too much of their money. It was costing more and more to support their lifesaving station and its activities in the manner to which they had become accustomed. They needed the funds to support their lifesaving station, so they stopped paying the professional lifesavers.

Many years later a member of the lifesaving station asked what their purpose was. "Why, of course," answered a member, "to provide a nice place for us and our families to fellowship, to have our community and social events. Why do you ask?"

Let me tell you another story. Once upon a time there was a society where people lived in the midst of immorality and didn't know Christ. Knowing that one of the by-products of a society undergirded by Christian values was a moral society, some Christians decided to build a church. ...

An Open Letter from the Devil

MARCH 2001

Hello. This is your friend the devil writing. I want to thank you for following my suggestions in the past. You have been a big help in what I'm trying to build. Let me remind you of some guidelines to follow. Your support has been a big help in the past and will help even more in the future.

First, never bring up, discuss, or preach on "controversial" topics such as abortion, pornography, gambling, drinking, sexual immorality, or any such private sins. Put your emphasis only on corporate sins. You can do so much more for me by doing that. Blame government and big business. Forget individual responsibility.

Don't worry about the moral character of our leaders. Just rate them on how good a job they are doing. Again I say, deal only with corporate sins, never with individual sins.

Don't get involved with controversial issues. Let someone else do it. Your plate is already full.

Always remember that there is no such thing as absolute truth. All things are relative.

Place spiritual issues at the bottom level of life.

Depend on the government to do things for you. Let them raise your children, educate your children, and train your children in right and wrong. Never criticize the social programs of government. Their experts are far more capable of solving problems than you are. Common sense can never compete against bureaucracy.

Never speak out on any issue using your Christian values as a perspective.

Don't get involved in politics. Don't run for office. Don't give any money or time to those who do. Don't let your Christian faith guide you in making your choices. Remember, we must keep the church and state separate. It says so in our Constitution, you know.

Keep listening to the liberal media. Let them fill your mind with their reporting day after day. By doing this, you will eventually come to agree with them. We all know they know what is best for our society. Remember that anyone who disagrees with them or tries to give a balanced perspective is nothing more than a member of a vast right-wing conspiracy. The liberal media can and will provide you with all the information you need to make the decision they know is best.

Remember the only thing necessary to be a good Christian is to go to church when you can, give a little money if you can. Remember that your faith should be a private matter between you and your church. Never try to apply it anywhere else.

You must remember to be tolerant of all others who think and live differently than you. Their lifestyle is just as good as any other lifestyle. All lifestyles are different but equal. Don't get involved in any kind of effort with any of the right-wing groups. They are oppressive.

Continue to ignore the Bible. It is an outdated book full of bad concepts. It is, you know, only a story of myths concocted thousands of years ago to keep the masses in line, to favor the male hierarchy and those in power. Like our Constitution, it is now out of date and useless.

There are many other suggestions I want to share with you later. I will write again. But for the time being, just keep following these. It will do a world of good for our common cause.

A Talk with God

OCTOBER 2001

Hello, God.

First, let me say that we appreciate all you have done for us since life began. You gave us guidance and help during our growing up period. You taught us about love and family and so many other good things. You really tried, but sometimes effort doesn't count. Times change, and now is the time for us to make a break from you.

God, we don't want to hurt your feelings, but we don't need you anymore. You really made a mess of things when you created us. However, we now have the knowledge and resources to clean up that mess.

Remember the fruit from the tree of the knowledge of good and evil you told Adam and Eve about in the beginning? You told them not to eat that fruit. But they did. And so are we. In fact, we are not only eating it, we are having a feast! And it tastes great!

We are in the process of developing scientific knowledge to make humans live hundreds of years. Scientists are close to extending human life to 200 or 300 years. Who knows, in the future we might live as long as Methuselah. And we can now create life, God. Using cloning, we are going to produce the perfect man. No disease. No deformities. Perfect, God.

We can even mix humans and animals to get the best of both. We can create the super race and then create a slave race to do our work. All we're doing is what you should have done many centuries ago. So we're going to finish the job you started – and do it right this time. We'll produce non-violent

39

beings that think like we think and do what we say. They will be whatever we want them to be.

Family? We've redefined it. No more one man, one woman stuff. We're free of the old moral constraints. Now family may be two men or two women. Three men and one woman. Three women. Any combination will be OK. No more nasty divorce. No more of this foolish commitment for a lifetime. You just don't get it, God. You never did.

And God, we've created very effective means of changing the thinking of humans. We have media mills on the East Coast and the West Coast, and they do a great job. We have our people in Hollywood and in the news media.

We can now build a perfect world.

Morals? We will determine those from now on. Your old set didn't work. They were too confining, too restrictive. Did you ever notice that the rules you gave Moses were all so negative? We're now more enlightened than you, and we understand what morals are best. That's another issue we can best determine for ourselves.

In fact, we have already eliminated your wrongheaded rules about sex. God, you made such a big deal about that, but sex is nothing more than another activity. So we have removed the limits you placed on it.

To be honest, God, you made a mess of things when you were creating. Now we have to clean up your mess.

What's that, God? Oh, we aren't worried about the institutional church. They are more concerned about the institution than the church. They spend their time keeping themselves going and don't have time to hinder us. It is no threat. In fact, we can even use the institutional church for our purposes.

How's that? A remnant of those faithful to you? Yes, God, that's about all you have left in the church.

To put it bluntly, God, we really don't need you anymore.

Sincerely,
Modern Man

Law of Love Constrains Christians to Confront

AUGUST 2002

Because of this, God gave them over to shameful lusts. Even their women exchanged natural sexual relations for unnatural ones. In the same way the men also abandoned natural relations with women and were inflamed with lust for one another. Men committed shameful acts with other men, and received in themselves the due penalty for their error.

Furthermore, just as they did not think it worthwhile to retain the knowledge of God, so God gave them over to a depraved mind, so that they do what ought not to be done. They have become filled with every kind of wickedness, evil, greed and depravity. They are full of envy, murder, strife, deceit and malice. They are gossips, slanderers, God-haters, insolent, arrogant and boastful; they invent ways of doing evil; they disobey their parents; they have no understanding, no fidelity, no love, no mercy. Although they know God's righteous decree that those who do such things deserve death, they not only continue to do these very things but also approve of those who practice them (Romans 1:26–32).

Forgiveness is one of the grand words in human language. Those who have gone before the Father in humility and repentance know that. In 1 Corinthians 6:9–11, Paul wrote to the Christians at Corinth:

[D]o you not know that wrongdoers will not inherit the kingdom of God? Do not be deceived: Neither the sexually

immoral nor idolaters nor adulterers nor men who have sex with men nor thieves nor the greedy nor drunkards nor slanderers nor swindlers will inherit the kingdom of God. And that is what some of you were. But you were washed, you were sanctified, you were justified in the name of the Lord Jesus Christ and by the Spirit of our God.

It is not the role of the church to justify sin, regardless of the sin. It is the role of the church, in the name of Christ, to confront and remind sinners that God forgives when there is humility and repentance.

We are engaged in a battle within the church today over the sin of homosexuality. Many, especially those in positions of leadership, want us to rewrite the Scripture so that homosexuality is not only condoned but blessed by the church.

If we are going to condone homosexuality, why stop there? Why not do the same with adultery? Stealing? Lying? Greed? You fill in the blank.

Samuel Langhorne Clemens, the agnostic better known as Mark Twain, once said it wasn't the parts of the Bible he didn't understand that concerned him, it was the parts he did understand. There are spiritual descendants of Mark Twain still around. They understand the Scriptures; they just don't like certain parts. So they reason, "Let us change those parts we don't like, and, thus, we can change the nature of God." Foolish thinking, but foolish thinking has been a trait of humans since they were created.

One thing I know. I don't just believe this; I know it. Our universe was created by a Creator. It did not come into existence by accident. It was created! It was created by an intelligent mind far beyond our ability to comprehend. And the Creator put certain order and logic into His creation. He made it plain that if we follow His order, it is good. If we deviate from His order, we suffer. It certainly doesn't take a rocket scientist to figure that out.

He made male and female different. And He did so for a reason.

We don't *help* people ... no, the statement should be stronger. We don't *love* people when we approve, bless, or condone a destructive, harmful, sinful lifestyle, be it homosexuality, adultery, thievery, dishonesty, greed, or any other sin.

Jesus once warned, "Watch out for false prophets. They come to you in sheep's clothing, but inwardly they are ferocious wolves. By their fruit you will recognize them ..." (Matthew 7:15–16).

I wonder who He was talking about.

The Building Called America

JANUARY 2003

Once upon a time a group of people decided to build a new building. It would be an unusual building, the likes of which the world had never seen. They decided that they would call this new building America.

Instead of having only one pillar underneath to support the structure as previous buildings once had, they decided that their new building would have three pillars on which to rest. Each of these three pillars would hold an equal weight of the building. They named these three pillars home, school, and church.

So the group began building their new building called America, and underneath they supported it with the three pillars of home, school, and church. The people labored on that new building until they died. But their children, catching a glimpse of the dream that their forefathers had, continued to work on the building and to keep strong the three supporting pillars.

Several generations worked hard to make that building the most treasured and admired building in all the world. They gave of themselves freely as they continued to work on the new building. And they always made sure that the supporting pillars of home, school, and church were strong. They knew that the existence of the building rested upon the strength of those three pillars.

However, several generations after the building was started, some people questioned the need of three pillars. They figured that it could stand on only two pillars. So they began to ignore the pillar of church. Soon that pillar became weakened due to neglect. When this happened, more weight of the building called America was shifted to the two pillars of home and school.

The people noticed that the foundation underneath the building called America was weakening. And they blamed many things, seldom referring to the weakened pillar of church.

Before long, because of the weakening of the pillar of church, the pillar of home became weaker also. This was followed by a weakening of the pillar of school. Many people tried to get the building called America on a good foundation again by strengthening the weakened pillar of church. But most of the people scoffed at them, calling them old-fashioned people with outdated ideas. The people tried many methods to strengthen the building called America, but none of the methods included the strengthening of the pillar of church.

One day this building called America collapsed. One of the residents crushed underneath the falling structure called out: "No building like America can ever stand except on the three pillars of home, school, and church." And with that, history wrote its final chapter on the building called America.

It this a true story?

Let's hope not.

I Am the Church

FEBRUARY 2003

I am the church. I work at a crisis pregnancy center. I help young girls and grown women seeking guidance on what to do with an unexpected pregnancy. I pray with them, counsel them, guide them, give them material support. I support them in their decision to give life to the unborn child. I weep when they do not. Yes, I am the church.

I am the church. I work in my community to establish standards that will help rid my community of pornography and obscenity. I complain to the elected officials. I work with them when the opportunity presents itself. I support laws that make it difficult for those who attempt to exploit others for monetary gain. I educate my friends and neighbors about the destructive nature of this material. Yes, I am the church.

I am the church. I promote the philosophy that society should be color blind, that a person should not be denied rights enjoyed by others simply because of the color of his skin. I do not believe that racism is practiced only by those of one color. I believe that in Christ there is neither Jew nor Gentile, slave nor free, black nor white (Galatians 3:28). Yes, I am the church.

I am the church. I am not afraid to be politically incorrect. I am not ashamed to proclaim that Jesus is the Messiah, and through Him and Him alone can our sins be forgiven. I do not believe that all religions are equal. Yes, I believe that Western civilization has progressed, making freedom more available and rights more equal, because of the Christian faith that proclaims that rights and responsibility go hand in hand. No, I am not ashamed of the gospel. Yes, I am the church.

I am the church. I do believe there is a moral standard that is higher and better, and that moral standard is based on the life and teaching of the one we call Christ. I do believe that when moral standards are relative and changing according to the whims of society, society suffers. Yes, I am the church.

I am the church. I believe that marriage is the divine plan of God, and that marriage is reserved for one man and one woman. I believe that anything other than God's divine plan is wrong, harmful, destructive, and – yes, I will use the word – *sinful*. Yes, I am the church.

I am the church. I am not a second-class citizen whose rights are circumvented simply because I am a follower of the Nazarene carpenter. I have the right to vote for those who share my Christian values. I have the right to apply those Christian values to any office in which I serve. I can and will apply my Christian values to the political process. I will render to Caesar the things that are Caesar's, but I will also render to God the things that are God's (Matthew 22:21). Yes, I am the church.

I am the church. I will not allow anyone to take me out of the mainstream and confine me to the four walls of a building. I will not be silenced by those with different opinions. I will stand for what is right as God leads me to see it, and I will not apologize for doing so. Yes, I am the church.

I am the church. I will continue to uphold the basic and fundamental time-proven teachings of the church that have contributed so much to making my country the most free place the world has ever known. And I will do so despite the fact that some highly placed "church leaders" use church dollars and church channels in their attempt to lead us into a "brave new world." Sin is still sin even when "church leaders" say it is not. Yes, I am the church.

I am the church. This world is not my home. I'm only passing through. I know that as long as I can apply and persuade others to apply the life and teachings of Christ to the world around them, we will help make society better for everyone. Yes, I am the church.

And I pray to God that I will continue to be the church for as long as I live. That will be my gift to the God who gave me the gift of life.

Persistence

MAY 2003

There is a story told about a certain little boy who wanted a watch. Day in and day out he pestered his parents about getting him a watch. His parents put him off every way they could. Finally he drove his parents to the breaking point. His father told the youngster that he didn't want to hear another word from him about a watch.

Well, for the rest of that week the lad said nothing about a watch. He knew that to do so would certainly bring some discomfort to his sitting-down place. However, Sunday soon rolled around, and the family was gathered together for a period of devotion. It was the custom in the family for each member to learn a new verse of Scripture and to recite it each Sunday during devotions. Every other member of the family had said his or her Scripture verse when it came time for the small lad to quote his. Looking up with a very solemn face, he quoted his verse, Mark 13:37, perfectly: "What I say to you, I say to everyone: 'Watch!'" Well, I'm not certain if he got his watch or the other thing. But one thing I can say for him is he was persistent.

And that's a quality all of us could use – persistence. One of our faults today is that we give up too soon, call it quits after a single setback, let failure break us instead of make us.

There is very little a person cannot do in this life if he sets out to do it and stays with it. One reason we don't accomplish more is that we are quick quitters. We get a setback or two, and then we say it can't be done. We give up. We quit trying.

But history is full of things that couldn't be done. And that means it is also full of people who did them.

The world looks up in admiration to a person who has staying power. He doesn't have to have great brains or great riches or vast opportunities. But if he believes in something and has the persistence to stay with that belief regardless of the praise or scorn he receives, the world ultimately will look up to him.

One reason there aren't more people with persistence than there are is the simple reason that it takes a big person to try again, to stick out the ship when the waves get high. Anyone can quit. Anyone can get into a lifeboat and float to safety. But the man with persistence is hunting neither safety nor another mission. He has something he wants to do, and he believes he can do it. So he stays with it, come what may. Then one day he finally accomplishes the impossible.

Great and good goals aren't easy to accomplish. They require great and good people to accomplish them. And great and good people are individuals who keep on keeping on. I believe God wants a person who says, "I can." I believe God wants a person who will try again.

"[A]ll things are possible" (Matthew 19:26). He is waiting to see if you believe Him.

If you do, stay with it.

Wouldn't It Be Nice?

JULY 2003

The young man was just becoming an adult. One day he sat down to visit with his grandfather.

"Gramps," the young man said, "I wish I lived in a country where we didn't have to lock our doors and windows all the time. Where we did not have to be fearful of someone breaking into our house and harming us. Wouldn't that be nice?"

"Yep," replied Gramps, "that would be nice. I know it would be nice because I lived in a country like that one time. In fact, in the house I grew up in we didn't even have a lock on any door or window."

"And, Gramps, I notice you always lock your car when you park it. You even have a security alarm so if anyone tries to get into your car, it goes off. Wouldn't it be nice to live in a country where you could leave your keys in your car if you desired and no one would bother it?" the young man asked.

"Yep," replied Gramps, "that would be nice. I know it would be nice because I lived in a country like that one time. I used to leave my car unlocked with the keys in the ignition."

"There's something else I would like, Gramps," the young man said. "Wouldn't it be nice if my friends and I weren't always tempted with so much sex in movies and TV? Why can't they encourage us to live a clean life like you and Grandma? Wouldn't that be nice?"

"Yep," replied Gramps, "I know it would be nice because I lived in a country like that one time. Entertainment was good and clean and wholesome."

"Gramps, wouldn't it be nice to live in a country where little babies were gifts from God and not simply a mass of tissue inside the womb? Where we didn't take the life of the most innocent, helpless members of our society. Wouldn't that be nice?"

"Yep," replied Gramps, "that would be nice. I know because I lived in a country like that one time. Society encouraged the mother-to-be to watch what she did and to watch what she ate and drank to make sure that the baby was born healthy," Gramps responded.

"Gramps, why can't we live in a country where couples stay married forever, like you and Grandma? Wouldn't it be nice to live in a country where everyone knew that marriage is between a man and a woman?"

"It sure would be," Gramps replied. "I lived in a country like that at one time."

"And what about being able to go to school where you were not afraid? Where students said 'Yes sir' and 'No sir' to their teachers. Where you said the Pledge of Allegiance each morning and you could pray and thank God for the food. Nowadays, Gramps, discipline is a real problem. At my school half of the students did drugs, and teachers were afraid to do anything because of the fear of being sued."

"That would be nice, Son. It would be real nice. I know because I lived in a country like that at one time," Gramps said.

"Gramps, I didn't know you ever lived anywhere but America."

"Son," Gramps said, "it was America. All these things and many more good things were a part of our life."

"But Gramps," the grandson said, "we live in America."

"I know, Son. But America isn't America anymore," Gramps said.

How Traveler Kept Traveling

NOVEMBER/DECEMBER 2003

Let me tell you a story.

Once upon a time there was a traveler who had a map. It was a good map. He could use that map to get where he wanted to go, even in territory not familiar to him. In any kind of weather, in any kind of conditions, that map would never change. It could always be trusted to be true. Traveler followed that map religiously when he traveled.

One day he wanted to go to a certain place. But as he traveled, he found that the road was rough. It wasn't smooth and easy like the interstate. This really didn't sit well with Traveler, so he got his map out again. Surely there was an easier road that would lead him to his destination. But, alas, he could find no other road on the map.

So he did what any experienced traveler would do. He chose a road that headed in the general direction and started down it. But the more he followed that road, the more it began to turn in another direction. Along the way he stopped to ask questions, to make sure he was headed in the right direction. Seeing a man by the road, he stopped and inquired of him. Traveler told him where he wanted to go.

"Sure," the man said, "this road will get you there. Just keep following it."

"But," replied Traveler, "have you ever been there by following this road?"

"Well, no, but I know it will get you there. Others – very intelligent people – have told me so," responded the man.

"What about going back to the main road and following my map again?" Traveler asked.

"Your map is old and worn out. It can't lead you to where you want to go. Only ignorant people still use that map. Enlightened people ignore the worn-out directions it gives," said the man, who was obviously very educated and experienced.

Well, Traveler kept traveling down the road, even though it seemed that he might not be headed where he wanted to go. Finally deciding that it might be time to return to the main road and follow his map, he saw a group. He stopped and asked them if the road he was on would get him where he wanted to go.

"Sure, just keep following the road, and you will get there," one in the group said.

"But have any of you ever followed this road to make sure it will get me where I want to go?" he asked.

"Well, no, but we all know that if you will follow this road, you can get to where you want to go," came the reply.

Upset, Traveler told the crowd that he was going back to where he left the main road and that he was going to begin using his map again. Upon hearing these words, the group began to berate Traveler for disagreeing with their wisdom. They called him such terms as stupid, uneducated, right-winger, bigot, homophobe, fundamentalist, even censor.

Now Traveler was so upset with this criticism that he ignored his instincts to return and use the map that had served him faithfully for many years. Traveler decided that to avoid the criticism and public humiliation, he had best continue down the road he was traveling. He did and continues to do to this day.

And he still hasn't arrived.

In fact, the farther he travels without his map, the farther he gets away from where he wanted to go.

Now, let me tell you another story. Once upon a time there was a church that had a Bible. ...

The Truth Hurts

FEBRUARY 2004

A friend of mind went to see the doctor some years back. He didn't want to hear what the doctor told him. And I doubt very seriously that the doctor looked forward to telling my friend the bad news. But he did tell him, and my friend did listen. He was told he had cancer.

None of us want to hear bad news. None of us want to believe it. But truth is true, and we best listen to it and act on it. Unfortunately, like Armenian King Tigranes the Great, if we don't like the message, we are often inclined to kill the messenger.

As we move toward the 27th anniversary of AFA, I guess it is time to reiterate something that I have said for the last 20 years. There is the possibility that I may make some, perhaps many, angry.

For me, the easy thing to do would be to ignore what I'm going to say. Just forget it. Why bother when I know that it will bring a negative reaction?

I do not consider myself a prophet. I do not consider myself to be wiser than others. I guess the only thing that sets me apart is that I have more than a quarter of a century of experience in dealing with the problem.

And just what is the problem? Basically, it is this: Our country is on a downward spiral of immorality like none we have ever seen before. Special rights for homosexuals have become the latest project for Hollywood and the liberal elite. Pornography fills our Internet, our TVs, our movies. Killing of the unborn continues unabated.

Drugs ravage our society. Promiscuous sexual activity is a game. Public education, to a large degree, is deteriorating in a continual exercise of political correctness. Violence is a means of resolving an argument or just an activity for sheer enjoyment. The institution of marriage is under severe attack. Religious freedom is in danger.

And who is to blame for this downward spiral? It isn't the pornographers. It isn't Hollywood or the liberal elite. It isn't Planned Parenthood. It isn't the people who make the guns. It isn't the people who run our schools. It isn't the drug dealers. They're only doing what is expected of them.

Unfortunately, we Christians are not doing what is expected of us.

As the comic character Pogo said, "We have met the enemy, and he is us."

Am I saying that we as individuals have caused all this moral decay? No. Absolutely not! But what I am saying is that we as Christians, collectively – members of the church – have retreated into our houses of worship and turned them into houses of comfort. Those of us who stand in the pulpit and sit in the pew have withdrawn from the public square so much and so often that we are no longer allowed in the public square.

Am I painting with a broad brush? Sure I am. Am I indicting everyone who calls himself a Christian? Of course not. But I am saying, taken as a whole, we have abandoned our responsibility to society.

Our efforts have basically been designed to make Christianity popular and comfortable. And in the process, we are no longer salt and light. We have built our buildings, hosted our activities, boasted of our numbers, and sought endless ways to entice people to join our church. We have, to a very large degree, turned our efforts to getting people into church instead of getting the church into people.

Is there still time to turn this ship around? Maybe. Maybe not. But one thing is certain. The church can't do it by following the path we have been on for the past half-century.

Am I writing this to make someone angry? No. Am I writing it with the hope that it will make someone take inventory and get involved? Yes.

Let me close by speaking to myself. You can personalize what I have to say if you desire. Individually I can't do everything. But I can do something. And by the grace of God I will do what I can. And I will start today.

Christians and Culture:
What Role Should We Play?

MAY 2004

How should we Christians respond to our society that is largely turning its back on the very values that have made the country great? Should we be involved in the political system to change laws and institutions so that they more closely reflect God's mind? Or should we only be concerned with changing hearts?

I believe the answer is that we should be waist-deep in both. As Christian activists we believe there is a biblical charge to restore our country to its godly foundation using the means that have been granted to us, means like voting and exercising our free speech rights to oppose those things that God opposes. At the same time, Jesus clearly tells us in Matthew 28 that evangelism and discipleship are priorities.

So, for American Christians who take the Bible seriously, we have two mandates to understand and to fulfill: restore our society to one that honors God, and at the same time, share with our neighbors how to find Christ and mature in Him.

And while we're doing all that, we must remember that our success is totally in God's hands. As I've written many times over the years, our duty is simply to be obedient.

Sure, we want to preserve a free world for our children and grandchildren. We want them to experience the same precious freedoms that we have enjoyed. However, in the end, all our efforts must be done in such a way that God is honored. That's how Jesus did things, according to John 17:4:

"I have brought you glory on earth by finishing the work you gave me to do."

Below are some questions for your Sunday School class or small group about a Christian's role in society. Search the Scriptures to learn what the Bible says about these questions. Then pray about what part you can play in making God's invisible kingdom visible here on this earth.

- If there is no God, can there be right and wrong?

- Has the church put as much emphasis on helping the needy in your community as it has on buildings and programs?

- Does the vulgarity in entertainment affect Christians as much as non-Christians?

- Do Christians have an obligation to vote?

- Should a Christian vote for a candidate based on the candidate's stand on moral issues?

- Does the message heard in Sunday School and during the worship service on an average Sunday make a difference in the day-to-day lives of most church members?

- Are the rights of Christians to speak out against homosexuality threatened by proposed "hate" crime laws?

- Would the government ever make it a crime to preach or teach that homosexuality is a sin? Would it do the same for adultery?

- Is there much difference in the lifestyles of the average Christian and the average non-Christian?

- Discuss the difference between "going to church" and "being the church."

- Is our society becoming more moral, less moral, or staying about the same?

- Is the child growing up in a single-parent home at a disadvantage? How can your church help?

- Is the United States a Christian nation or a secular nation?

- How does the dominant religion of a country impact its civic and cultural life?

How to Build a Football Team

MAY 2005

Once upon a time there was a small group of people who became interested in football. They loved the excitement and thrill of football. So they gathered one day and made a decision to build a football team.

Now they knew that in order to build a football team they first had to know the rules. So they went out and bought a *Rule Book* for every member. Then they began to study the *Rule Book*, making sure that they fully understood the rules so they could be successful on the field.

They began to meet regularly to study the *Rule Book*. For one hour each week they would meet, take out their *Rule Books*, and proceed to go over every section and subsection. Soon they decided that one hour a week was not enough time to learn the *Rule Book*, so they added a second hour each week. In fact, they wanted so much to have a good football team that they even began studying the *Rule Book* another hour each week. So for three hours each week, they would meet and study the *Rule Book*.

Knowing that others were also interested in football, they invited them to become part of the team and attend the *Rule Book* meeting. Soon the little group began to grow. Because of the growth, they had more funds to apply to studying the *Rule Book*. They invited outside experts to come to their meetings and explain the intricate parts of the *Rule Book*.

They studied the rules concerning defense, offense, passing defense, passing offense, how the linemen should posture themselves on both offense and defense, how the members of the backfield should line up, how long they had to snap the ball, how many officials were required to officiate the game, how they should block on offense and defense, how to tackle, how much movement there could be on the line of scrimmage, and all the other various and sundry rules of football in the *Rule Book*.

They even started printing the *Rule Book* with leather covers in different colors (red, blue, black, etc.) for different groups (*Rule Book for Hunters, Rule Book for Teens, Rule Book for Moms*, etc.). They added a concordance, defensive and offensive patterns, and even a cross-reference.

Day after day, week after week, month after month, they continued to study the *Rule Book*. In fact, many of the members could quote nearly the entire *Rule Book* from memory.

They eventually decided it was time to hire a coach. When the coach attended his first meeting with the potential football players, he was utterly amazed at the vast store of knowledge they all had of the *Rule Book*.

One day, after they had met to discuss the *Rule Book*, the coach asked them when they wanted to start practicing and playing.

"Practicing? Playing? What's that?" the group asked.

The coach was stunned. "You know. Practicing so we can get prepared. And playing. You know. When do we have a game?"

"Oh no, coach," one of the team members said. "You misunderstood. We are here to study the *Rule Book*. That's our top priority. We just want to make sure that we know the *Rule Book*."

And with those words, the coach walked out the door. After all, he was looking for a team that wanted to play, not one that only wanted to study the *Rule Book*.

And that is the story of a group who wanted to build a football team.

That reminds me of another story. This one is about a group of people who wanted to build a church.

Once upon a time ...

Church at a Crossroads:
Competing Worldviews

AUGUST 2005

Editor's Note: Dr. Wildmon was talking about worldviews long before the phrase became common. This column is condensed from his address before a Chicago gathering of U.S. church leaders March 23, 1987. In it, he defined truths that have become even clearer today.

We are in the midst of a spiritual war, not only in our country but in Western civilization. This spiritual struggle is between two opposite and competing views of the world and humankind. One view is what can best be described as the Christian view of man. This view says that God is God and man is man; God loved man so much that He gave His only Son to suffer and die for man's sins; we are created in the image of God; and our worth is based on the fact that we are God's children and not on anything we have done to deserve God's love.

The other view of the world and humankind has several names – secularism, materialism, humanism – but, in essence, it says that the God of the Christian perspective doesn't exist, and if He does exist, He doesn't matter. Simply put, this other view says that man is his own god, and no other god, if there is one, makes any difference.

It is my premise that the problems of our culture have come about largely because the church has refused to accept its responsibility to lead in areas where it has a right to lead and is expected to give leadership. Consequently, our society now finds itself at a crossroads. Sitting squarely in the middle of the crossroads is the institutional church. In our current moral crisis, the church – and only the church – has the resources to maintain the Christian view of humankind as the foundation for our society.

What must the church do? First, it must effectively educate its constituency as to what secularism and materialism are and the values this worldview espouses. If we are to maintain a society where the dignity and individual worth of each person is held in high esteem, then we simply must educate our people as to the differences between the Christian view of man and the other view.

Next, the church must make a commitment, collectively and individually, to address the problem, pay the price, and fight the fight with the intent to win. We must call our people to follow Christ and emulate His love for truth and righteousness and His intolerance of evil in their daily lives. We must encourage our people to become active in the political process – to run for office, to work for candidates, to vote.

Then, we must encourage the members of our individual church bodies to take specific actions such as writing and calling companies that support pornography and/or sex, violence, and profanity on television. We should encourage our members to join in organized boycotts of companies that refuse to respond to moral persuasion.

Finally, our efforts should begin immediately by calling the church to education and action. To delay will only bring more suffering, hurt, and brokenness. I call you to commit yourself and your influence to this struggle. If we are successful, those who come after you will rise up and call you blessed.

Faithfulness Brings No Regrets

MARCH 2006

Back when I was a parish minister and regularly preparing sermons, I would often find poetry that spoke to me. One such poem that has stayed with me over the years was written by Ella Wheeler Wilcox. Let me share it with you.

One ship drives east and another drives west
With the selfsame winds that blow;
'Tis the set of the sails
And not the gales
That tells them the way to go.

Like the winds of the sea are the winds of fate,
As we voyage along through life;
'Tis the set of the soul
That decides the goal
And not the calm or the strife.

Looking back on nearly three score and ten years, that poem still rings true.

We are given one life and one life only to live. We make our choices and arrive at our destinations.

With the help of my parents and others who touched my life, I was fortunate enough to discover that truth at a young age. So I made a decision to use that one life as a follower of Christ. It was the wisest decision I ever made about anything.

The years have come and gone. They shall never return. I have invested this life in trying to follow where God calls.

Had I followed my own preferences, I would have gone another way. If I had my druthers, I would have rather been given another type of ministry, one where I could have been a hands-on participant in helping the poor and needy. One where I would have gone to my little corner to serve and only a handful of people would have ever heard my name.

But God, in His wisdom, had other plans. He put me down in the very middle of a raging culture war. It was a ministry of confrontation where decisions were not always between black and white but often tinted with gray.

But I thank God there was a place where He could use me. And I thank God for the privilege of serving him in the capacity to which He called me.

Whatever lot God chooses for your life, follow it. It may not be the one you want, but it is the one He has given. When He says for you to take up your cross and follow Him, do it.

Life will be richer because of it.

Safety or Salvation?

FEBRUARY 2007

The following story is from the book *Horns and Halos in Human Nature* by Dr. J. Wallace Hamilton published in 1954.

There is a very old story about a church that needed new hymnbooks. A patent medicine company very generously offered to print the new hymnbooks in return for the privilege of putting their advertising in them. But instead of placing the advertisements on the back page or even on the front page, they mixed it up throughout the hymns. On Christmas morning when the books were presented, the pastor stood up and read the first verse of the first hymn:

> *Hark! The herald angels sing,*
> *Beecham's pills are just the thing;*
> *Peace on earth and mercy mild,*
> *Two for man and one for child.*

That is a pretty silly story, but something like it has really happened to the good news of God as it has come down through the years. The clear truth of it has become badly mixed up with the thing it started out to conquer. When you look at the historical expression of Christianity across the years and across the lands, salvation for multitudes of people called Christians has come to be little more than a craving for protection, a device to insure safety from hell and the punishment of sin without saving them from sin.

We have inherited, and still hold in our minds, certain mechanical theories of the atoning work of Christ that give altogether too much encouragement to those who want the benefits of the cross without the battle, who want safety without spirituality, who look to God to change their legal relationship without changing *them*.

We all have listened to some evangelist speaking on the topic of what a person must do to be *saved*. And before he got far, we knew that what he really was talking about was what a person must do to be *safe*. There is a difference there.

What did Christ come to do?

Certainly, He did not come to bring safety. Nowhere do you hear Him say, "Follow me and you will be safe." He said, "Follow me and you will get a cross." (That's my paraphrase of Matthew 16:24.) He did not come primarily to save us from the consequences of sin. He came to save His people from their sins – that is, to cure the evil in their hearts, to make them different. He didn't come to get us into heaven. He came to get heaven into us.

Without Christian Ideals, Democracy Dies

MARCH 2007

Arnold Toynbee once said that if you want to study comparative religions, buy a ticket instead of a book.

What the famous historian was saying was that you learn more about a religion by seeing what practical effect it has on a society.

We are at a critical point in the history of our country and our world. Two religious perspectives stand in stark contrast with one another, each desiring that its religion serves as the basis of our values. Islam and the Judeo-Christian faiths are clashing because adherents of both want their beliefs to serve as the foundation of cultural values and because of the divergent paths being used to pursue their goals.

Unfortunately, many, if not most, of our leaders do not realize that there is a vast difference between these two value systems.

It is my opinion that our leaders don't understand the difference in the way the Eastern mind and the Western mind function. One wants forced submission to Allah achieved by the sword; the other desires voluntary submission to God achieved by a changed heart.

In one respect, 9/11 was the best thing that ever happened to Islam. That day cast Islam into the mainstream of religious debate. Prior to 9/11, we would refer to Christians and Jews when speaking of religions in this country. Now we speak of Christians, Jews, and Muslims.

In one way, you could say that ancient Greece was the forerunner of democracy. But it was the teachings of Jesus, permeated throughout the Western mind, that made the soil fertile for democracy to grow and flourish.

Have there been some dark moments in the history of Christianity? Of course there have been. But to define a religion, one must turn to the standard of its teachings, not to isolated events. This is true of Judaism, Christianity, and Islam.

If nothing else, perhaps our current situation will force those of us who choose the Christian value system to re-examine our religion's core principles. It is going to be absolutely necessary to do so if our system of democracy is to continue.

The conflict we are experiencing will be around for a long time. It will not be resolved in a matter of months, but years – if it is ever resolved.

I would suggest that our churches go back to teaching the basic fundamentals and we Christians spend much time examining our faith. If we don't understand the basic fundamentals and how our faith plays out in the real world, we will lose this war of ideas.

And with it goes our democracy.

The Power of One: AFA's Familiar Refrain

MARCH 2008

We received an email at the office a few days ago from a supporter in South Florida. It's the kind of email that keeps me going on days when I'm discouraged or would like to give up. He and his wife run a sales and service business. He's the cubmaster for his son's Cub Scout pack. And he's running for Congress.

He wrote:

I do not really consider myself a deeply religious man, but I do believe in God and Jesus Christ. I receive your emails regularly and have sent emails when I have felt inspired by your words. I have emailed Ford Motor Company several times, once directly from their website. I wanted to see if I got a response. Not yet.

I was just reading your article titled "What Can One Person Do?" I felt that I needed to email you. I am one of those who have felt compelled to run for political office as you suggest – to see if one man can change things. I live in South Florida where liberal politics seem to rule. I have written my congressman several times about issues, some of which you alerted me to. My last letter to him was about H.R. 3685 – adding sexual orientation to the discrimination laws. His response was basically that we all need to be more tolerant.

That was the final straw when I decided I was going to take his job if at all possible. I have never been in politics and frankly never considered it, but I believe I can do a better job than this man is doing. The ongoing assault on Christianity nationwide and the systematic removal of God from everything really must be stopped. It will destroy the moral fiber of this country that I love.

I wanted to let you know that you are at least somewhat responsible for my pursuing this course of action, and I wanted to thank you for your continued efforts.

Through the years, I've written and spoken a lot about what one person can do in the culture war: cultivate a genuine concern, be informed, pray, be a faithful church member, support your pastor and urge him to address moral issues in your community, organize a social action task force in your church or neighborhood, write letters to the editor of local and regional newspapers, get involved in political campaigns, distribute literature, and spend your money with moral responsibility. The list could go on and on. Be creative in finding ways to make a difference.

I've always said we shouldn't leave politics to the politicians. Our Florida friend is this month's Exhibit A, a visible symbol that should motivate others to get involved.

Now we've taken a look at his campaign website, and we don't agree on every issue. Even so, I commend him for deciding that he needs to try to make a difference. I hope his example challenges you to get involved in politics at some level. If our Judeo-Christian culture is to survive, your community, your state, and your nation need you.

Not Ashamed

"For I am not ashamed of the gospel, because it is the power of God that brings salvation to everyone who believes: first to the Jew, then to the Gentile" (Romans 1:16).

In literature there is a figure of speech called a *litotes*; it expresses a positive principle by stating it in negative terms. For example, I feel pretty sure that in Romans, Paul was saying not only that he was "not ashamed" of the gospel, but also that he took pride in the gospel. The right kind of pride – not boastful or arrogant pride and self-importance, but reasonable and justifiable respect.

That's the way I feel about these truths that I've been thinking of and jotting down over the last few days. Not only am I "not ashamed" of these truths, but I also take a certain measure of pride (reasonable and justifiable, I believe) in them.

I am a Christian, and I'm not ashamed of it.

I am an American, and I'm not ashamed of it.

I am a conservative, and I'm not ashamed of it.

I am pro-life, and I'm not ashamed of it.

I believe marriage is only for one man and one woman, and I'm not ashamed of it.

I vote my convictions, not a political party, and I'm not ashamed of it.

I don't buy anything I cannot afford, and I'm not ashamed of it.

I believe the baby in the womb is a person, and I'm not ashamed of it.

I believe sex is not a product for sale, and I'm not ashamed of it.

I believe our schools should educate, not indoctrinate, and I'm not ashamed of it.

I believe judges should judge, not legislate, and I'm not ashamed of it.

I believe in school choice, and I'm not ashamed of it.

I believe the best welfare program is a home with a mother and father, and I'm not ashamed of it.

I believe our Constitution, not the laws of any other nation, should be the sole source for legal decision-making, and I'm not ashamed of it.

I believe the liberal media are big-time biased, and I'm not ashamed of it.

I believe capitalism nurtured by Christian ethics is the best economic system for any society, and I'm not ashamed of it.

I believe socialism will make us all equal (equally poor), and I'm not ashamed of it.

I believe that those who preach tolerance are the most intolerant individuals you will ever meet, and I'm not ashamed of it.

I believe those who refer to others as bigots are the real bigots, and I'm not ashamed of it.

I believe I have one earthly life to live, and I intend to live it fighting for those things I believe.

And you know what? I'm not ashamed of it.

Why Eagles Fly, Chickens Flutter

JUNE 2010

Once upon a time, a long, long time ago, the eagle and chicken were very good friends. Everywhere they went, these friends went together. It was not uncommon for people to look up and see the eagle and chicken flying side by side through the air.

One day, while flying, the chicken said to the eagle: "Let's drop down and get a bite to eat. My stomach is growling."

"Sounds like a good idea to me," replied the eagle.

So the two birds glided down to earth, saw several animals eating, and decided to join them. They landed next to the cow. The cow was busy eating corn but noticed that the eagle and the chicken were soon sitting on the ground next to her.

"Welcome," said the cow. "Help yourself to the corn."

This took the two birds by surprise. They were not accustomed to having other animals share their food quite so readily.

"Why are you willing to share your corn with us?" asked the eagle.

"Oh, we have plenty to eat here. Mr. Farmer gives us all we want," replied the cow.

So the eagle and the chicken jumped in and ate their fill. When they finished, the chicken asked more about Mr. Farmer.

"Well," said the cow, "he grows all our food. We don't have to work at all."

"You mean," said the chicken, "that Mr. Farmer simply gives you all you want to eat?"

"That's right," said the cow. "Not only that, but he gives us shelter over our heads."

The chicken and the eagle were shocked! They had never heard of such a thing.

They had always had to search for their food and work for shelter.

When it came time to leave, the chicken and the eagle began to discuss the situation: "Maybe we should just stay here," said the chicken. "We can have all the food we want without working. And that barn over there sure beats those nests we have been building. Besides, I'm getting tired of always having to work for a living."

"I don't know about all this," said the eagle. "It sounds too good to be true. I find it hard to believe that one can get something for nothing. Besides, I kinda like flying high and free through the air. And providing food and shelter isn't so bad. In fact, I find it quite challenging."

Well, the chicken thought it over and decided to stay where there was free food and shelter. But the eagle decided that he loved his freedom too much to give it up, and he enjoyed the consistent challenge of making his own living. So, after saying goodbye to his old friend the chicken, the eagle set sail for the wild blue yonder.

Everything went fine for the chicken. He ate all he wanted. He never worked. He grew fat and lazy.

But then one day he heard the farmer say to his wife that he was yearning for fried chicken. Hearing that, the chicken decided it was time to check out and rejoin his good friend the eagle. But when he attempted to fly, he found that he had grown too fat and lazy. Instead of being able to fly, he could only flutter. So, the next day, the farmer's family sat down to chicken dinner.

When you give up the challenges of life in your pursuit of ease and security, your ability to fly turns into a flutter.

And that's the reason eagles fly and chickens flutter.

Like Father, Like Son

JULY 2010

Written about 1967 ...

My study was located in a storage room directly behind our home. It was a very small room to begin with, and once I put my books and supplies and machines in it, I could hardly turn around.

One day I was having one of those days when everything seemed to go wrong. My desk was covered with matters that needed my attention, correspondence was lagging, and there were other matters pressing.

I was sitting in my study, half-mad at myself and half-mad at my lack of space. Then, without knocking, in came my son Timmy, who proceeded to sit down behind me. I started to turn and tell him there wasn't room for him, but I waited, for I knew that if I spoke at that moment I would be harsh with him. So I went about my work, listening as he began taking paper from the wastebasket and books from the shelf.

"Daddy," he said, "do you have a pen?" I reached into my pocket and gave him my pen. I then tried to continue my work. But it seemed that every time I turned around I bumped into him. So, my temperature rising, I turned to scold him and send him back into the house. Upon turning, I was stopped cold by what I saw!

Timmy had laid out some old papers from the trash can, some of my books, and with pen in hand, he was marking on a sheet of paper. He had made himself a makeshift desk that was in something of a mess.

Now most of the time when Timmy wants to know what I'm doing out in the study, I tell him, "I'm studying." I looked at him there; he paused for a moment and looked up, and after thinking a few seconds, he began to write again.

"What are you doing, Son?" I asked.

He looked me in the eye as only a son can do and gave me his answer with a little grin on his face: "I'm studying, Daddy."

I didn't say anything else to him. I turned back around and pretended to go back to work. But I didn't do much work for the next few minutes. I just sat there thinking how proud I was of my son. It made me feel just as big as a man can get knowing that my son wanted to be like me – to do what I do.

But then a greater truth came to me. My Creator was telling me that this was really what He wants from me. He wants me to be like Him. How good He must feel when we act like Him, do what He does, and live like we are His children. "Wouldn't it be a good world," I thought to myself, "if we wanted to be like Him as much as Timmy wants to be like his father?"

Fast-forward to July 2010 ...

Today, as AFA leadership moves from my shoulders to Tim's, I'm prouder of my son than ever before. I am confident in his heart, his desire, and his abilities to lead AFA where God would have it go. Godspeed, Son.

APPENDIX
An Interview with Don Wildmon

By Rebecca Davis and Hamilton Richardson
Updated from the September 2007 issue of AFA Journal

Seventy-seven years old, Don Wildmon still makes his way into the office daily. He's not as young as he used to be; his dark wooden cane aids his stride at times. His workdays are shorter, his eyesight blurred, but his purpose sure. It's another day in the life of American Family Association, and "Bro. Don" is determined to be part of it. For 40 years, Wildmon, in some way, has been on the front lines of America's culture war.

In 2009, the Lord brought him through a 123-day hospital stay because of Saint Louis encephalitis that he contracted from a mosquito bite. That near-death illness was followed by the diagnosis and surgical treatment of cancer behind his eye. God spared his life, and Wildmon presses on, remaining faithful to the call God placed on his life to form AFA in 1977.

Here, Wildmon goes behind the scenes of AFA and inside the rooms of his heart to reveal the man and the mission behind the ministry.

What is the story of Don Wildmon prior to AFA?

When I was nine years old, I felt the Lord calling me to be in ministry. When I was about 18, I decided that God was calling me to the pulpit ministry. I tried that for a year or two. Being an imperfect person, I found it very difficult to preach to people. I didn't really understand God's grace, so I left the parish ministry. I didn't want to ever go back to it. So it was rather frustrating to feel like there was something you should be doing and not knowing what it is you're supposed to be doing.

I spent a couple of years in the Army. I finally decided one day that God had called me to preach, that I should go back into the ministry. The Lord and I debated it. I tried to get into seminary, but they wouldn't let me in because they said I couldn't pass the courses based on my bad college grades. I went through college just loafing, never really putting forth any big effort. So I went to a couple of influential people who came in on my behalf, and the seminary decided they would give me a test. If I could pass that test, they would admit me. I'm assuming I passed the test because I went straight through seminary – finished the three-year program in two years and three summers and finished with about a 3.2 grade point average.

What prompted you to begin AFA?

With our four children, Lynda and I were watching TV one night during the Christmas season in 1976. There were only three networks at the time, and all three had objectionable material. I can't even remember the programs. I remember one was violent. Another had a sexual scene, and the third one had profanity. I decided fighting this is what the Lord had called me to do, and I began at that point.

What was your first step?

I had been in journalism nearly all of my life. I had studied media, and I came up with this concept of "Turn The Television Off Week," which was just turning it off for a week. I knew it would grab the attention of the media because it had all the background for good media play. Here's this small-town preacher who thinks he's going to do something to influence television. I played the game in order to get the publicity in order to get the word out. The media gave me a good bit of publicity for a while until it became evident that "hey, he just may be able to pull this thing off or do something." The media backed off and began the attack game, which has been going on ever since.

What was the first name of your organization?

We named the organization National Federation for Decency. When we began, we were primarily dealing with television and pornography. Over the years, a lot of the left-wingers would make fun of our name. So I changed it in 1988 from National Federation for Decency to American Family Association because our concerns had expanded, and it was very hard to demean the word family back then.

When you first started was this a full-time effort?

This was a full-time effort from day one – 16, 17 hours a day, nearly seven days a week. I had to do everything myself, but work has never bothered me. I traveled a good bit and ran the ministry out of our dining room with a desk and a phone and a small offset press I bought with my own funds. I went two and a half years before I had any help at all. But my wife Lynda was very supportive. She, in fact, went back to work teaching soon after I began the ministry. I was paid a salary of $1,800 a year the first year that AFA began.

Did you get support from your church?

I was still a pastor when we first began, and they were supportive with "Turn The Television Off Week." Soon after that, I made the decision to leave the parish ministry, and as far as my denomination, I can't remember anything they did. I can remember a few times when they opposed what I was trying to do. In the early years, the most critical letters I received came from fellow pastors who were telling me "God is love" in letters that had hate oozing off the page.

What is the church's problem?

It's probably a combination of many factors. We've had at least one generation, maybe two now, to grow up on television. And they've seen millions of commercials, and they've heard the liberal/secular message since they were kids, and there's a weakness in the church. The church has not really dealt with the basic fundamentals much. The church has isolated itself, and I'm not so sure it hasn't forgotten its mission to be salt and light.

What is AFA doing in response to this?

We're trying to inform people who want information. We're trying to involve people who care and want to get involved. We're trying to impact the culture around us. The church ought to be doing all of those things. Unfortunately, too often, the church's success is measured by buildings, budgets, and baptisms.

How has God blessed AFA?

The older I get, the more evident it is that God has been behind this ministry. He's brought good people who are willing to work hard. I remember one time when I was struggling financially. I had sat down that morning and figured up that I owed $5,000. I didn't have $5,000. I didn't know where $5,000 was coming from. That afternoon I got a call from a businessman. We talked, and he said, "Well, you're doing good work, and I'm going to put you a check in the mail for $5,000." A year later, I was again in debt $5,000. Didn't know where the money was coming from, and I don't waste money. I squeeze the penny. I got a call from another businessman. I didn't even mention it [my debt]. He said, "Oh, by the way, my wife and I just put a check in the mail to you for $5,000." There have been a few things like that. Has God directed this ministry? I think he has despite all my faults.

What Christian leaders have supported AFA over the years?

We've had support from many Christian leaders who shared our concern: Larry Burkett, Marlin Maddoux, William "Bill" Bright, Jerry Falwell, Adrian Rogers, Phyllis Schlafly, James "Jim" Dobson, and D. James "Jim" Kennedy. All my old buddies are dying off, and I'm not getting any younger myself.

Who are some of the people behind the ministry?

In the early years, all the people who came to work for AFA were giving up their security, because we were young. We are non-profit. We didn't have deep pockets. My first paid employee was Larry Durham, who was in charge of data processing and is still working here. My first employee was our volunteer bookkeeper Forest Ann Daniels, who later became the second employee on the payroll. We began publishing a monthly newsletter that turned into what is now the *AFA Journal*. Six years after the ministry was founded, Randall Murphree came to work for us as editor of the *Journal*. I consider that a God thing because he's been around, and we now have a very excellent monthly publication. As for our supporters, we still don't have a lot of major contributors. We have maybe two or three people who give us around $100,000 to $200,000 a year. But other than that, our donations have come from small gifts, primarily. To be honest with you, I would prefer it to be that way.

How did American Family Radio become a part of AFA?

I came up with the idea of using radio after reading *Broadcasting Magazine* for another reason. I came across this little item about how the FCC was going to allow you to send your signal by satellite, and that opened up a whole new world. So we began a strategy of building translators, small repeater stations. That was a God thing.

Where do you see AFA in the future?

I don't know, but I would expect the ministry – unless it loses its orientation – to be much larger and more effective. You're called to be faithful, not successful. You go on with the hope that you haven't lost the culture war, with the hope that you can still win it. Your responsibility is to fight the battle. The outcome is not in your hands.

What has been the most difficult challenge over the years?

The failure to convey to the church the situation that we're in. In fact, I spent 15 years or longer trying to do that.

Finally, I said it's not going to happen, so I quit working with it. There's nothing you can do. The church is there. It's asleep. People in the church have jobs and families and school and everything else, and this doesn't touch them directly right now. It will later. But I'm afraid that by the time they realize what's happening, it may be too late.

Do you ever feel like giving up?

I've felt like quitting. In the early years, I argued with the Lord many times. Nearly about took what religion I had out of me. It did shape some of my views over the years, but that was the most difficult period I had to go through. People that I felt should simply be 100 percent behind Christian morality were the ones who wrote the most hateful mean-spirited letters to me about love.

Why do you press on?

I press on now through my son Tim who took over the ministry's leadership in 2010 because this is what the Lord called me to do. Look, when it's all said and done, nobody here is going to say this or that about Don Wildmon. One of these days, I'll see the Lord, and I can honestly say I did the best that I knew how. I think that's the answer that He wants.